A Vision of Hope

The story of Samuel Habib, one of the Arab world's
greatest contemporary Christian leaders and his plan
for peace in the strife-torn Middle East where the
Cross and Crescent meet and where the Bible, Koran
and Torah vie for centre stage.

David W. Virtue

Foreword by Tony Campolo
and
Preface by Samuel Habib

regnum
Oxford
Akropong, Buenos Aires
Irvine, CA, New Delhi

First published 1996 by Regnum Books International in association with
Paternoster Publishing, P.O. Box 300, Carlisle, Cumbria CA3 0QS UK

Regnum Books International

P.O. Box 70, Oxford, OX2 6HB, UK

17951 Cowan, Irvine, California, USA

P.O. Box 76, Akropong-Akuapem, Ghana

Jose Marmol 1734, 1602 Florida, Buenos Aires, Argentina

Post Bag No. 21, Vasant Kunj, New Delhi 110057, India

02 01 00 99 98 97 96   7 6 5 4 3 2 1

British Library Cataloguing in Publication Data

A catalogue record for this book is available from the British Library.

ISBN 1-870345-16-9

Typeset by WestKey Ltd., Falmouth
Printed in Great Britain by BPC Wheatons Ltd, Exeter

Acknowledgements

I wish to thank Dr. Samuel Habib for allowing me the opportunity to write this book on his life and ministry and for making himself so available in the midst of his enormously busy travel schedule. He and the staff of CEOSS graciously gave of their time to let me see and experience the work of CEOSS in Egypt first hand.

I also wish to thank Sue Eedle, who spent endless hours with Dr. Habib and who graciously transcribed tapes for me. Mention must also be made of Rafik Habib, who gave me deeper insights into his father's life and character and who helped me understand some of the intricacies of the Arab mind.

Thanks must also be extended to Andrea Stephanous who, while briefly studying in the United States introduced me to Dr. Habib and excited my interest in his life and ministry. Andrea and his wife Hala graciously extended to my wife and me the hospitality of their home while we were in Cairo.

My gratitude also goes out to the Rev. John and Betty Hendrickson for reading the manuscript and making helpful and critical observations that made the book just that much more readable. They are more than just my in-laws.

Finally to my wife Mary, who read the manuscript and whose critical comments helped refine the text and make it a better book. Her determination kept me going when the writing, at times, seemed difficult.

David W. Virtue
West Chester, Pennsylvania.

Preface

This book was started before the historic peace accords were signed between the Palestinian people and the government of Israel. The agreements struck between the two peoples promise a new era of hope and peace in the Middle East that has not been seen in more than half a century. The future looks more promising now than at any time in modern memory. Historic enemies for the first time shook hands before a watching world, across a divide of hatred and fear. It was an occasion that will go down in the annals of modern political history, a moment never to be forgotten.

In Egypt, the Coptic Evangelical Organization for Social Services has, for years, been working in support of the cause of social justice, one of the main tools of peace in the Middle East.

While peace treaties bring hope of a better future for the region, peace on paper between former enemies has to be cemented by practical expressions of peace within ordinary communities. This has been a key part of CEOSS's mission since the 1950s, and today has greater relevance than ever before.

Samuel Habib, General Director
CEOSS

Contents

Egypt

BACKGROUND

Egypt is a country with a rich past struggling towards a better future. Few countries in the world can rival the riches of its ancient civilization and archaeological findings. The fascinating monuments left by the Pharaohs, Greeks and Romans as well as by the early Christians and Muslims trace a long and glorious history.

But like most Third World countries, Egypt shares the frustrations endemic in its struggles. Its future hangs in the balance. Egypt must modernize its economy before the 21st century if it is to feed its fast-growing population of nearly 59 million people, nearly half of whom live in urban areas. Egypt is now the most populous country in the Middle East and the second-most populous country on the African continent. Ninety percent of its people are Muslims; ten percent are Christians.

The country itself is about the size of Texas and New Mexico combined, almost 387,000 square miles, with an economy that is basically agricultural, being one of the world's largest cotton producers. Egypt receives financial assistance from the World Bank and the International Monetary Fund as well as from the European community and the United States as it embarks on a politically risky programme of economic reforms that will, in the short term, significantly increase unemployment and possibly fuel inflation.

Internally, the pressure is on to control the rapidly growing population which adds an additional one million mouths to feed every nine months. This puts an enormous strain on the country's already overcrowded inhabitable, largely urban areas. In the past ten years Egypt's population has increased by thirty percent.

In the political realm Egypt has played, and continues to play, a pivotal role in Middle East politics. It was a party to the Camp David accords which resulted in the first diplomatic relations being established between Israel and an Arab nation. Its role in the Arab world is symbolized by the eventual relocation of the headquarters of the Arab League to its original premises in Cairo, after a 12-year hiatus in Tunis following Camp David.

Egypt has since assumed a behind-the-scenes mediating role between the Arab world and the United States, and played an essential part in bringing about the 1993 peace accords between Israel and the Palestinian people.

The country, however, faces its own internal crises. Fundamentalist extremists within Islam threaten the civil order and the rights of the Christian minority in Egypt. Their aim is to overthrow the present government of Hosni Mubarak and turn Egypt into a strict Muslim state similar to the Khomeini regime in Iran.

These fundamentalists have targeted the government as well as moderate Muslims, some Christians and tourists in their campaign of violence, the purpose of which is to create a sense of dissatisfaction among the people in the hope that they will vote the government out of power, if not topple it by force. In the meantime their activities have severely hurt the once burgeoning tourist industry, the country's primary source of foreign revenue.

The Egyptian people as a whole are not happy with all of this, and with their co-operation the government has been trying, with some success, to regain full control of the situation. Although the rise of fundamentalism poses an acute challenge to the government and people of Egypt, Christians and Muslims alike continue to feel and emphasize that they are all citizens of one nation, having lived and worked together for centuries. And while Egypt faces problems and growing pains, there are every day positive signs of hope, progress and improvement.

Foreword

By Tony Campolo

A BALANCED MAN IN AN UNBALANCED WORLD

It's hard to be a prophet and to be balanced at the same time. But balance is exactly what is needed for a prophet of God, and in every sense of the word, Samuel Habib is such a man. As one of the foremost leaders of the Christian community in Egypt, he has tried to live out a golden mean amidst those who articulate extremist ideologies and would lead Egypt into self-defeating courses of action.

Samuel Habib has had to deal with unbalanced extremists within the Christian community itself. On the one hand he has had to stand up to those fundamentalists who would limit the mission of the church to a pietistic salvation that gets people saved for heaven. On the other hand he has had to keep from getting swallowed up by a Protestant liberalism that would reduce Christianity to an array of social improvement programmes.

Against both of these extremes Samuel Habib proclaims a holistic gospel. He preaches a Christ who came to deliver humanity from *all* the consequences of sin, and he knows that those consequences are manifested both on the individualistic and societal levels. As an evangelistic preacher, he knows the importance of calling people to commit their lives to Christ and find in him both the deliverance from sin and the empowerment to live out the will of God in the world.

But this man is sufficiently attuned to the message of Christ to realize that the effects of sin are evident not only in the 'lusts of the flesh' but are also evident in the 'principalities and powers' which dominate social life. He preaches the Kingdom of God and knows that that Kingdom is defined as transformed people living in a transformed societal order. His message is the good news about a Christ who is at work in us and in our world, making all and everything new.

It is this holistic Gospel that has informed Samuel Habib's action over the years. He has not compromised the declaration of a Christ who transforms souls, nor has he given ground to any who would leave social activism outside of being a disciple of the Lord.

II

The Christian community cannot be defined by the simple categories of the fundamentalists and the liberals. Other divisions also must be considered. There is the ancient Coptic Church, the Roman Catholic Church, and the Protestant community. In Egypt each of these three groups of Christians at one time or another have stood in opposition to each other.

Such sectarian bickering is particularly destructive to the Christian Faith in a nation where Christians compose only ten percent of the population. But Samuel Habib has not let the broken body of Christ escape therapeutic efforts. More than anyone else in Egypt he has brought together leaders of these three branches of Christendom, and has endeavoured to make them into a co-operative mission that reaches out with the whole gospel to the whole Egyptian community.

It is seldom that a prophet is able to be simultaneously an agent of reconciliation, but Samuel Habib *is* such a prophet. He is well received by all three branches of Egyptian Christianity, and he has been able to unify them in a variety of social ministries. It was Samuel Habib who organized the Coptic Evangelical Organization for Social Services (CEOSS). This is the largest social service agency in his country, and it has a brilliant record of organizing Christians in literacy programmes, entrepreneurship projects, agricultural programmes and medical care. His effectiveness in creating and administering this nationwide organization has drawn worldwide attention.

Samuel Habib's most daring efforts to bring about religious reconciliation, however, lie with what he has been able to negotiate with the Egyptian Muslim community. While fundamentalist extremists in the Islamic community seek to purge the land of anything that is not Muslim, Samuel Habib has reached out to those moderate Muslims that make up the majority of the Egyptian people and tried to make some peace. While recognizing that there are beliefs and commitments that will always separate Muslims from Christians, he also knows that it is possible to establish a spiritual kinship between these rival religions. He knows that the peoples of these two major world religions can and must learn to live together for the good of their nation.

It just may be that in modelling his unique style of co-operation between religions, while still maintaining theological integrity, Habib may be demonstrating an arrangement that can be imitated around the world. We all know that unless Christians, Muslims and Jews can learn to live out their respective convictions in the context of love and peace, the future of our world is bleak.

The former president of Egypt, Anwar Sadat, dreamed of such a co-operative future, and to that end he proposed that on a hill overlooking the Sinai that there be constructed, side by side, a Jewish temple, Muslim mosque, and a Christian church. He dreamed of what Habib is helping to make happen – social unity in the midst of religious diversity.

III

Samuel Habib's penchant for social justice is informed by some brilliant cross-cultural perspectives. He recognizes that Egypt's alliance with the Palestinian cause has brought to his people economic disaster, war, and social chaos. But while he sees all the problems of being aligned with the Palestinians on the one hand, he is more than cognizant of the injustices perpetrated on the Palestinian people by the state of Israel. He is also aware of how decisions made by the United Nations have caused suffering and humiliation for the Palestinian people.

It's hard for those of us in America to imagine what it would be like to have some international parliamentary body meeting in some far off country, making decisions that would deny us our rights and cost us the land on which we live, but that is just what happened to the Palestinians when the United Nations declared that the Jews would have a homeland. The Jews who have been the most oppressed people in history, have, in respect to the Palestinian people, become oppressors. Against such injustice the voice of Samuel Habib can be heard.

To further complicate matters, Samuel Habib's commitment to justice for the Palestinian people sets him in diametrical opposition with some of the strongest beliefs held by American fundamentalists. He does not hold to the dispensationalist theology that has a commitment to clearing Palestine for the Jews as a condition for the fulfilment of Biblical prophecy. Instead, he believes that the *New* Israel, referred to in the Bible, is not a political entity, but one composed of those – Jews and Greeks, bond and free, Scythian and Barbarian, and all others – who by faith become part of the Body of Christ.

For Samuel Habib the church is the new Israel. And while he sees the creation of a nation-state for the Jewish people as an inevitability which may have some good consequences for history, he does not see the restoration of the state of Israel as a precondition for the second coming of Christ. Everything that needs to be fulfilled for Christ's return is already fulfilled, so far as he is concerned. Christ, he contends, can return at any moment, and this parousia does not require the establishment of a new nation in the Middle East or the reconstruction of the temple on Mt. Zion to make it happen. Considering the extent to which fundamentalist-dispensationalist dollars and missionaries undergird Christian ministries in such Third World nations as Egypt, the fact that Habib is willing to differ with them on what they have made a crucial part of their eschatology is evidence of great courage.

IV

As a sociologist, I am most intrigued with the commitment of Samuel Habib to social change. Assuming what H. Richard Niebuhr refers to as 'The Christ, The Transformer of Culture Posture', he believes that the salvation of God in history requires that as core to its mission the church participate in changing the world into a more just political-economic system. He has no overly optimistic illusions about what we can achieve, but he is convinced that the calling of the church is to do all that is possible to move society in the direction of becoming the Kingdom of God.

In this book you will have ample evidence of his struggle to effect change in Egypt. Courageously he has stood for the rights of women, even when it meant defying traditional taboos and customs. You will find in Samuel Habib a man whose commitment to justice has translated into policies and programmes that have aided the poor.

But even in his efforts to bring justice to bear on society, Samuel Habib charts the course of the golden mean. For while he has the passion of a revolutionary, he also has the good sense to know that the practices of revolutionaries do not usually make for progress towards democracy and equality.

Samuel Habib has been able to reject the extremist cries of liberation theologians. While he is intrigued and in agreement with their critique of societal iniquities, he does not find among the liberation theologians a viable plan of action that will work for Egypt. He turns from those Marxist ideologies that he rightly discerns lead to totalitarianism. Instead, he goes the route prescribed by Max Weber, that German sociologist who called for change to come through economic development and education programmes that provide slow but steady evolutionary social transformation. It is not surprising, therefore, that Samuel Habib has spent his life creating the kind of programmes that are suggested by the Weberian scheme.

A man like Samuel Habib is a rarity, and that's why this book is worth reading. As someone who teaches in the field of community development, I have found the life of this man more than just fascinating. This man is a model. He is what Weber would call "an ideal type". I believe that he exemplifies the best balance of those qualities, beliefs and ideas which are essential for someone committed to nation-building.

This is not just the record of a good man living out his faith. This is the story of a man who has some answers for people everywhere who look at our desperate and shattered world and are trying to find ways to put it back together again.

Tony Campolo
Professor of Sociology
Eastern College
St. Davids, PA

Introduction

In the constantly turbulent Middle East the detached onlooker can sometimes find it hard to detect any rays of hope. Yet there is light amidst the darkness of political and religious struggles, social inequities and oppressive regimes. People of courage and vision are patiently nurturing hope and working towards that light.

One such man is the Rev. Dr. Samuel Habib, General Director of CEOSS, the Coptic Evangelical Organization for Social Services, based in Cairo, Egypt. Habib is a man with a mission and a vision.

Forty years ago, as a young man in his mid-twenties, raised in a solid middle-class home with parents in the Evangelical (Presbyterian) church, Samuel Habib made a faith commitment to serve Jesus Christ. During his teenage years he came into contact with the Society for the Salvation of Souls, a non-denominational evangelistic movement active in some of Egypt's major cities at that time. This opened his eyes to the deep spiritual needs of those around him and pushed him inescapably towards Christian service.

Deeply moved by his experience and the critical needs, both spiritual and social that he saw among his people, young Samuel Habib entered the Evangelical Theological Seminary in Cairo, convinced of God's call on his life. Such a commitment, he knew, would be total and irrevocable. He had chosen for God. It would be a lifetime call.

A VISION OF HOPE is the story of Samuel Habib, Christian peacemaker, visionary, evangelist and ecumenist, who for more than a quarter of a century has waged peace, seeking social justice and development in the face of seemingly hopeless odds.

Now, it seems, peace is in the air. A Palestinian Arab leader and an Israeli head of government have shaken hands across a chasm of ideological differences and, for the first time since Israel was granted statehood, Palestinians inside the occupied territories have been granted the right to run their own affairs.

Peace is not total harmony, it is true, but it is the beginning. The

Middle East will never be the same again. Two enemies, at bitter loggerheads for decades, have sat down at the table of peace. What has taken place fundamentally alters the political and psychological landscape of the region as nothing else has done.

Based in Cairo, Samuel Habib has watched as his own country has gone to war with Israel, with devastating results. Now he watches with profound sadness as his country is racked with violence, torn by defiant and fractious Islamic groups who seek to overthrow its government.

This story is about God's call on Habib's life, the birth of CEOSS, and the powerful impact his ministry has on both Christian and Muslim communities in Egypt.

At times Samuel Habib rubs shoulders with the poorest of the poor, some of whom can be found living on Cairo's oppressive garbage dumps. At other times he sits down with Egypt's highest political and religious officials to discuss ways of fighting illiteracy or improving health care conditions and the overall quality of life for Egypt's teeming millions.

As head of the Protestant churches of Egypt, Samuel Habib treads judiciously and diplomatically among different Protestant groups, the seven Catholic churches in Egypt, the Coptic Catholic church, and a handful of Orthodox churches (Syrian, Greek and Armenian, for example) and the Coptic Orthodox church, which is the largest of all the Egyptian churches in size and power.

He is always mindful, too, that ninety percent of his fellow-citizens are Muslims and that he must serve the needy among them as Jesus would, with love and compassion. Samuel Habib recognizes the inherent dignity of all people and, while many do not share his commitment to Jesus Christ, he has been called to be a seeker of social justice, serving all his fellow-Egyptians without partiality or prejudice.

This is the story of a man who is both prophet and pragmatist. It is also the story of CEOSS, an organization whose work embodies the vision and mission of this gentle but tenacious man.

Samuel Habib is, above all else, a theologian of hope. This is his story. It is a story of profound hope and joy in the midst of at times almost insurmountable problems and difficulties.

Chapter 1

Years of Preparation

Samuel Habib rose from behind his desk and stood quietly facing the Coptic Orthodox priest. Outwardly he was calm, inwardly he was deeply anxious. Before him stood a black-robed cleric shaking with rage at the editorial he had just read in *Message of Light*, Samuel Habib's development magazine for new literates. In it the young man had dared to challenge the centuries-old practice of female circumcision performed on young girls by Christians and Muslims alike. And now here he was being confronted on the stand he had taken by a village leader who was also a cleric of the mainstream Christian church in Egypt. It was a moment of reckoning. Would Sam back down or would he stand firm on this and a whole host of other issues that confronted and enslaved millions of Egyptian women, and in so doing face overwhelming personal and community opposition? Sam stood his ground.

It was May 1956 and this would be the first of many battles Sam would have to face over the course of a lifetime of Christian service. He knew confrontation was going to be a part of his life, an inevitable part, one even fraught at times with danger. But Sam saw himself as an agent of change, an agent of reconciliation, serving his Lord and Master in the face of immense opposition, no longer willing or able to close his eyes to the painful practices that dehumanized millions of Egypt's women.

A new day was dawning in Egypt, and Samuel Habib was about to play his part in seeing that the morning light would shine more brightly in all the dark places bringing healing and reconciliation to all who clung so precariously to life along the Nile.

Samuel Habib was born in the city of Wasta, 50 miles south of Cairo in the province of Fayoum in Middle Egypt, on February 28, 1928, the eldest of six children. Six months later, his father, Habib Sourial Morcos, a civil engineer, and mother, Mounira Yanni Saleh,

moved the family to the city of Tahta in the province of Suhag in
Upper Egypt, 280 miles south of Cairo. It was there that he spent
his formative years. Sam could trace his family tree back over several
generations and, like the Biblical record of generations, he is in turn
the son of Habib, son of Sourial, son of Morcos, son of Girgis, son
of Henein. Both his parents were from solid, conservative middle-
class families in Middle Egypt, and their home provided a modest
level of comfort and security for a large and growing family.
Samuel's younger brother Fouad, a science graduate, later moved
to the United States to live, marry and work. Of his four sisters,
Zuhoor is a housewife, Yvonne, a government lawyer, Amal, a
history teacher and Nawal a pharmacist. They are all married and
live in cities throughout Egypt.

Samuel Habib's education began in a government-run primary
(elementary) school, followed by a private secondary education in
his home town of Tahta. He was considered an excellent student
and athlete, and his ability as a runner earned him a visit to the
provincial capital of Suhag to receive an athletic prize from the hand
of King Farouk, the reigning monarch of Egypt.

The system of education in those days consisted mainly in
learning facts by rote and then passing stiff, dry examinations based
on the amount of information one could absorb and regurgitate
back to the examiner's satisfaction.

Sam did, however, study the English language which was later
to stand him in good stead, and also French. But he found the
education system unappealing to him, as it did not encourage either
creative or critical thinking, and he was more than happy to move
on to studies that demanded more philosophical inquiry and
reflection and which better suited his cast of mind. His later studies
would prove to be far more stimulating and mind-broadening.

Sam was brought up in a Christian family within a predominantly
Muslim neighbourhood. His parents were Christians, as were his
grandparents and great-grandparents. Samuel Habib's Christian
heritage could in fact be traced back, like that of many Egyptian
Christians, to the first century when the first Christian missionaries
crossed the Sinai Peninsula into Egypt.

His parents had formerly belonged to the indigenous church of
Egypt, the Coptic Orthodox Church, one of the oldest churches
in the world, which traces its origins to a group of Egyptian Jews
who attended Pentecost in Jerusalem, were touched by the Holy

Spirit and returned to Egypt committed to spreading the Good News about the promised Messiah.

Later, his parents joined the growing Evangelical Church which had been established in Egypt in 1854 by Presbyterian missionaries from the United States. Through aggressive nationwide evangelistic campaigns, the Presbyterian Church grew and flourished during the late 19th Century, beginning first in the cities of Cairo and Assiut gradually spreading across the country making converts and building new churches. Today, renamed the Evangelical Church in Egypt, the churches boast half a million members with 300 congregations and eight presbyteries.

Sam's father became an ordained elder in the local church, under the leadership of the Rev. Zaki Grace. His administrative and organizing abilities were quickly recognized and soon put to good use. It was into this church that Sam was born and raised. From his earliest childhood Sam faithfully attended Sunday School and was taught to read the Bible. He became active in the life of the church as well as the community. He lived and breathed the air of Christian faith within his close and tight community, always surrounded by the wider circle of Islam and the daily call of the minaret.

His mother was by nature a peacemaker, a reconciler between friends and, if necessary, between the children and their father who, as the family patriarch, could on occasion be somewhat dictatorial over minor issues. On matters of principle, however, there was no compromise by either parent. While he could not have foreseen it, his mother's peacemaking qualities would later spill over into Sam's own diplomatic activities as a peacemaker among contending religious groups and with political leaders in his native Egypt. The seeds had been sown. His future life would be marked by the need for compromise and diplomacy.

But it was the manner in which his father conducted his personal life that most deeply affected the young man. He saw how his father, a leader in the community, stood by his principles even if it hurt and at times endangered him. Sam watched with awe as his father boldly said what he thought and felt and openly challenged those who would attempt in business dealings to bribe him. He repeatedly saw his father put principle ahead of profit in his business affairs.

His father's concern for people also spilled over in the way he conducted himself in the very Middle Eastern tradition of hospitality.

Sam recalls his father's practice of hospitality, taken at times to extremes. He was a man of tremendous generosity and deep personal concern for people. If someone came to their home, or had a need that he heard about, Habib Sourial would drop everything to attend to that person. Whether it was someone in the church, in business, in their social circle, or who had neither status nor money he would move everything to help them. He placed relationships above everything else. He would sit for hours listening to people's problems, offering advice, even giving away his hard-earned money to help those who were in need. His priority was always people, his generosity overwhelming. Watching his father at work sowed further seeds in young Sam in how he would conduct his later life.

Sam claimed his father's generosity and concern for people as his own heritage, but later changed his thinking about how he would use his time in helping people, following his education in the United States.

His father would, in later years strongly disagree with his young son's 'advanced' thinking on how much time should be devoted to hospitality as opposed to organizational matters. At times he would grow angry at his son's unwillingness to drop everything to attend to callers, which the father perceived as indifference to people.

It was, in reality, simply different perspectives between the generations, brought about by changing times which neither man could control.

Another illustration of the minor differences between them, was in the matter of movie-going. Habib Sourial did not agree with people attending movies, his son included. Sam felt otherwise, and on occasion went to see a film. They agreed to disagree.

Habib Sourial was the archetypal family patriarch, and when he held a strong opinion it was almost always impossible to change his mind. Yet on theological and Biblical issues in particular he would be open to discussion, and the two men would talk seriously for hours about current issues of the day and the different attitudes and practices of the various Christian denominations.

In this very significant area Sam's father was the teacher par excellence. Habib Sourial was an ardent churchman and an active layman, regularly preaching in his own and other churches in and around the city of Tahta. He was a man with strong evangelical and ecumenical convictions open to working with all kinds of people and nurturing relationships with the leaders of many different Christian churches and groups.

Despite his strongly-held opinions he was not a narrow-minded man. He would attend meetings at Coptic Orthodox and Catholic churches and had many friends in both denominations, while at the same time remaining loyal to the Evangelical Church to which he and his family belonged.

Habib Sourial also had numerous Muslim friends, whom he dealt openly with in business. Sam's father was impatient and intolerant of small-minded people and had no time for narrow-minded and prejudiced thinking.

In those days, tensions ran high among the various churches and denominations in Tahta. It was not uncommon to hear preachers rail against one another from their pulpits on Sunday morning on various points of doctrine and faith: the Orthodox Church railed against the Evangelical and Catholic Churches; Catholics railed against Protestant, and Protestant against everyone else.

Denominational lines were sharply drawn even in the local public schools Sam and his brother and sisters attended. There were occasions when they faced criticism from teachers and students simply because they attended the small Evangelical Church in Tahta.

Young Sam watched as his father tried to establish relationships with members of the two large Orthodox churches and the Roman Catholic Church in the city. Despite the tensions and animosities that were always present, Sam saw in his father a model of Christian character, profound faith and deep commitment that left an indelible imprint on his young mind.

This affected not only the way he thought but also his own goals and aspirations, and the way he would handle himself in difficult situations that would arise in his own future. His father's diplomatic skills influenced his elder son in ways that he could not have foretold or imagined for the young man.

On the whole, the Christian community in Egypt in the Thirties and Forties was very pietistic and inward-looking, distancing itself from the political and social life of the country. It was felt by most Christians that to be socially or politically involved meant compromising one's faith. To show any interest in political affairs meant that you were either not a Christian or not a very spiritual person. People would show concern about what was going on in the

national life of the country but they never got involved politically.
Nor was it the case that Christians were excluded from politics or
public life on the basis of their beliefs. The truth was that Christians,
in their piety, withdrew themselves from the political arena into
the privacy of their lives and refused to become involved. Business
yes, politics no.

Habib Sourial nevertheless believed in exercising his right to vote
within the fledgling democratic process in Egypt. He read the
newspapers and listened to the radio learning what he could of the
political issues of the day. But he never got actively involved in
politics himself, preferring to work as he did within his community,
striving for change at the local level.

He would, however, listen intently to news about the activities
of the various political parties; the corruption of the king and those
around him in the royal palace, and the misuse of the nation's
wealth. He listened with awe and pride as colonialism drew to an
end with the evacuation of the British military presence from Egypt.
These were heady times for the nation and for young Sam as he
watched his country change.

As a teenager in the early Forties he took only a passive interest
in the issues of the day, but he actively followed the political
fortunes of the nationalist Wafd Party and avidly read their daily
newspaper. Sam was always interested in political news and soon
became engrossed in Egypt's changing political climate. He enjoyed
the liveliness of Egypt's budding democratic life, the freedom of
the press, and the liberty people were given to express themselves
and criticize any and everything, except, of course, the monarchy.
But the main focus of Sam's life was the family and the local church.
With little or no social life in Tahta, and no parks or playgrounds
to go to, the church and its activities filled Sam's leisure hours and
became his whole life.

He was always aware of the relative strength of the various rival
churches in Tahta and beyond the city, and he felt disappointed
and frustrated that his own local Evangelical (Presbyterian) Church,
located in a relatively poor section of town, was so feeble and lacked
vision.

Even the more recently founded Holiness Movement Church
was stronger than the Evangelical Church in Tahta. This and the
Christian Standard Church, another branch of the Holiness Movement, both established by Canadian missionaries at the turn of the

century, were very pietistic and inward-looking, but they had a spiritual vitality he could not ignore.

While still a student in secondary school, Sam was eager for his church to be more active. He was encouraged in this by his father's habit of thinking big, and by the preaching and fiery sermons of the powerful evangelical preacher Rev. Dr. Tawfiq Gayed, pastor of the largest Evangelical Church in the nearby provincial capital of Suhag. The Rev. Tawfiq Gayed drew large crowds to hear his powerful exposition of the gospel and his forthright attacks on the Coptic Orthodox Church. Sam would frequently travel to Suhag just to hear the famous preacher. It was through him that he learned to respect the Evangelical Church, its theology and witness.

But these were difficult days for the struggling Protestant churches in Egypt, most of which had been in existence less than 100 years. Egyptian Christians, though a minority, took great pride in the history of their martyrs. While this is the primary focus of the Coptic Orthodox Church, both Catholics and Protestants consider it part of their heritage as well. Their forefathers kept the gospel intact and preserved Christianity in Egypt in the face of enormous persecutions throughout history.

Surrounded by the overwhelming history of the Orthodox and Catholic churches in Egypt, the fledgling Protestant Churches struggled to find their place in Egyptian society. Despite his father's best intentions to forge bridges between the churches, Sam's early years were times of profound struggle as he listened to them fighting among themselves, and while he found joy in his faith and drew strength from his father's spiritual vitality, the theological battles being fought by the churches and different denominations deeply troubled him.

Sam threw himself into the life of his local church and became active in all its ministries. During his adolescence he methodically read through the Bible in its entirety once a year with the help of Arabic commentaries, carefully taking notes as he read. He saturated himself in the Scriptures which formed the basis of nearly all his thinking. His knowledge of the Word was the guiding force behind his later call to the ministry. Just as Paul wrote to Timothy, Sam from his youth knew the Scriptures which had made him wise unto salvation.

His religious upbringing deeply influenced the way he thought and conducted his life. His younger brother and four sisters also followed their parents' example. For them, to possess faith was as natural as eating.

But it was his Old Testament namesake, the prophet Samuel, who led Israel to victory and who had anointed Saul and David, who was most often pointed out to him as an example, and with whom young Samuel Habib developed the most spiritual kinship. The prophet became his model and guide.

Over time, it became obvious to those around him that something very profound was going on inside the young man. A deep spiritual battle was being waged. As Sam listened to the Christian faith being expounded week in and week out by Egyptian Protestant preachers, a tiny seed was being sown in his own young soul.

Towards the end of his secondary education he began to sense the call of God on his life in a very special way. By the time school ended he knew he wanted to go into the Christian ministry. The powerful influences that had been shaping his life had taken hold. God, he believed, had spoken and had laid His divine seal of approval on Samuel Habib's young life. Years of Bible study and prayer had left their indelible imprint on his life. He would no longer be his own man, he would henceforth be God's true man, doing God's will, in God's time, in God's way.

In the late Forties, while still a teenager and a member of the local Evangelical Church, he was invited to join the Society for the Salvation of Souls in Tahta. This was a non-denominational lay organization established in 1927 by Egyptian nationals actively engaged in evangelism and Bible teaching. Through this ministry thousands had been converted to Jesus Christ, and the society had attracted members from all three branches of the Church - Orthodox, Catholic and Protestant. The society's focus was the preaching of salvation by faith alone in Jesus Christ through revival meetings.

While the society was not registered as a church and did not administer the sacraments of Baptism and the Lord's Supper, its active evangelistic programme attracted Sam, and he joined the new branch that had opened in Tahta as a result of the revival going on in the town. It was in this organization that young Sam hoped to find what he had not found in his home church, namely an opportunity to become a more active Christian and witness for Jesus Christ.

When he joined the society his gifts were soon recognized and he quickly became a leading member full of enthusiasm and ambitious ideas to advance the cause of Christ that some of his more timid colleagues did not always fully share or support. Nothing, it seemed, could hold Sam back. Even at the tender age of 15 he saw a vision of how things could be, and he was determined to press ahead with the changes he envisaged.

To begin with, he immediately made a move to transfer the society from a small building it was currently housed in to a larger compound right in the heart of Tahta, and promptly announced an ambitious campaign to build up its activities.

Sam argued in favour of holding a series of open-air meetings in a large courtyard with the capacity to seat 500 people. His colleagues opposed the idea, saying that he would look foolish if only fifty showed up. Undeterred Sam immediately began a vigorous publicity campaign, and when the first night of the evangelistic rally rolled around the courtyard saw a full house with standing room only.

Overwhelmed by the response, society members ran around town the next day looking for more chairs to seat the growing crowds they expected the following evenings.

The meetings attracted people of all ages and all walks of life. People were hungry to hear the word of God. People yearned to know more about the Bible, as much of the preaching offered in their own local churches failed to satisfy their deepest spiritual yearnings. They longed to hear the plan of salvation explained simply to them.

While Sam witnessed all that was happening, there were other stirrings going on inside of Sam as well. Egyptian society was, at that time, a deeply segregated society, especially between the sexes. There was very little intermingling between men and women in public places. For example, almost all the churches in Egypt had a screen down the middle of the church, made of wood or masonry, sometimes more than six feet high, separating men from women. The two groups were made to sit on opposite sides of the screen and were not permitted even to see each other. This may well have been a throwback to forms of worship in the Jewish synagogues which also saw men and women separated from each other.

In this instance women would not normally be invited or expected ever to attend public meetings such as the ones Sam and his friends were planning, but Sam wanted to change all that. In an unprecedented move, he invited both men and women to the gatherings. The decision to do this sent shock waves through the community, and so to placate the city's leaders and public displeasure the society erected a high screen between the men's and women's sections of the seating area.

Tahta was still a very conservative community, and Sam had no wish to upset the whole town.

He was told bluntly by other society leaders that women would never attend the meetings anyway. They were culturally conditioned to obey their leaders. However the invitation went out nevertheless inviting all to come.

To his utter surprise, and to the amazement of his sceptical colleagues in the society, more than half of those who turned out to the next and subsequent public meetings were women. In fact people of all ages and walks of life appeared, regardless of gender or religion. A deep spiritual hunger was apparent everywhere. Many men and women and not a few youth were converted to Christ through these evangelistic campaigns.

In later years, as a leader of the Protestant churches in Egypt, Sam campaigned energetically and successfully, despite much opposition, to having the screens separating the sexes removed from Evangelical churches around the country. This aroused considerable misunderstanding and hostility, and he made a number of enemies in the process. Over the course of time, however, he won the battle. Today all Evangelical churches in Egypt have removed these screens. Many still have men and women sitting on opposite sides of the church, with an open aisle between them, but the screens have gone.

While these battles were being fought inside the Protestant churches, there were other changes going on outside of the church that were beginning to shake the foundations of Egyptian society. The outside world was beginning to encroach on Egypt's timeless traditions in numerous small and large ways. One of those was in the area of dress codes.

At that time most women still wore the traditional long dresses and black wraps that covered them from head to toe. Faces were either partly or totally veiled. Sam's mother and sisters, however, were among a small but growing group of women who chose to abandon this tradition and wear Western-style clothing.

This was a fundamental break with tradition. Centuries-old clothing styles were designed so as never to provoke sexual arousal in men. Certainly nothing about his wife's Western-style clothing should do so.

Sam had no desire or interest in blazoning forth the provocative edge of Western fashion styles. Increasingly Egyptian women, including his wife, chose the more tasteful and tailored forms of Western clothing. Sam saw no contradiction in any of this nor did it seem offensive to Egyptian society as increasingly his country came in contact with the West. Consequently his mother and sisters saw no ambiguity nor were they embarrassed to wear Western clothing and accept the changes.

Early in life Sam had been taught to respect not only the uniqueness of women as being made in the image of God, but also their freedom to express themselves as uniquely God's creation. To hinder their growth was to fail to treat them as equals. He saw this from his reading of Scripture and the way his father treated his mother. This understanding of women's freedom later spilled over into other areas of Egyptian culture and life regarding age-old sexual practices affecting women that he found particularly abhorrent. In those days, in a closed society like that of Egypt, in fact in most Arab countries, Sam's thinking was revolutionary and years ahead of his contemporaries.

For now, though, Sam threw himself energetically into the activities of the Society for the Salvation of Souls, while at the same time voraciously reading all the Christian literature he could get his hands on, mostly drawn from his father's extensive personal library of biblical books.

Among the many volumes he read and studied were the biblical commentaries of Dr. Ibrahim Sa'id, an Evangelical scholar and preacher noted for his elegant use of the Arabic language and for his public oratory. Sa'id was editor of the non-denominational Nile Christian Publishing House, as well as being pastor of the largest Evangelical (Presbyterian) Church in the Middle East. His commentary on the gospel of John has since been recognized as a masterpiece of interpretation and erudition by the international biblical community.

Sam devoured practically every theological book available in Arabic, including books published by the Egyptian Society for the Promotion of Christian Knowledge, an Anglican publishing house. In fact the writings of Habib Sa'id, an open-minded Egyptian Anglican became the cornerstone of Sam's library and thinking.

Habib Sa'id's books on the Life of Jesus and the Apostle Paul, written in the late Forties, are still highly regarded by Egyptian Christians today.

Sam's wide reading provided him with the content he needed for his expanding calls to preach and speak in Tahta and the surrounding towns. From Tahta he would regularly travel to Suhag and Assiut preaching on behalf of the Evangelical Church and the Society. Sam was slowly being recognized as a man with a mission and with gifts the church could use.

When he first sensed God's call into full-time Christian service, Sam found little support from among his friends; indeed even he himself resisted the idea. Many of his supporters told him he could carry out his work as a witness to Christ equally well, if not better, as a lay person, favouring the idea that Sam should study medicine. His colleagues in the Society did not feel it was necessary to devote one's life to the institution of the church in order to do God's work.

But he had sensed God's call to enter the ministry, and that was what he decided to do. Only his parents fully supported his decision, though his pastor, the Rev. Zaki Grace, also believed in Sam's call and encouraged him. Despite the scepticism of his friends the call to ministry would not go away.

A very deep part of Sam knew he had been called by God to serve his people. He had no real idea of how, or what it was he was being called to do, but the call to serve was nevertheless very clear. The general will of God for his life as revealed in Scripture was clear enough. To walk the life of faith in obedience and godliness was without question his first call. To discern the particular will of God for his life was a much harder task.

Was it the success of his activities in the Society for the Salvation of Souls, or the weakness of the Evangelical Church in Tahta, that drew him on? Whatever it was, compelling forces inside Sam told him something had to be done within the church to revive it, to move it forward off of dead centre.

Sam's roots lay in the local church. He had quietly moved from the non-denominationalism of the Society towards inter-denominationalism, while still holding on to the essential truths of the gospel. His primary loyalty was always to his Lord, but it was the Evangelical Church that he wanted to see revived and flourishing.

There was now no going back. Sam had heard the call and

heeded it. Over the course of time Sam would discover his calling to be on a scale infinitely wider than he could possibly have imagined. He stepped out in faith. God would have to do the work through him to accomplish his will. While he had no definite plans as to what he would finally end up doing, he knew that whatever it was he needed to be fully trained and theologically prepared.

And so it was that in the summer of 1947 he presented himself to the Presbytery in Suhag, the provincial capital, and took the exam to gain admittance to the Evangelical Theological Seminary in Cairo.

In September 1947, at the age of 19, he entered the seminary to study theology for the next three years, by now totally convinced of God's call on his life. That sense of calling marked him out as a future leader. He would not disappoint either his heavenly Father or his earthly family. Nothing now would turn him back.

Young Sam Habib was one in a class of five. Intellectually gifted and eager to learn, he threw himself totally into his theological studies, marking himself out early as one of the most aspiring and hard-working students at the seminary, hungry to read all the books he could lay his hands on in the few short years he had for full time study. If he was to rightly divide the word of truth for his people he first had to learn how to do it for himself.

The seminary proved more than adequate to the task and provided Sam with the necessary theological climate to explore the mysteries of God.

The Evangelical Theological Seminary in Cairo, established in 1926 under the auspices of the Synod of the Nile of the Presbyterian Church was the oldest Protestant seminary in Egypt. Later it came under the control of the Evangelical Church of Egypt, supported totally with Egyptian funds.

The first presidents were Presbyterian missionaries from the United States, but when Sam joined the seminary the president was an Egyptian, the Rev. Dr. Gabriel Rizkallah. A number of the professors were American missionaries, though, and this gave Sam his first exposure to the ways Westerners thought and to Western theology. The seminary was also bilingual. Teaching was done in both Arabic and English.

The seminary provided a sound theological education and training in pastoral work for the budding theologian, and included the study of Greek and Hebrew, the origins of the Bible and Biblical criticism. In addition, Dr. Boutros Abdel-Malik, a seminary professor who also taught at the American University in Cairo, encouraged Sam and three other seminarians to take some classes there. Driven to learn as much as they could, Sam and his friends enrolled concurrently in the Faculty of Arts and Sciences at AUC. Dr. Malik taught the ancient languages of Syriac, Hebrew and Aramaic at the American University's School of Oriental Studies, where the four seminarians took courses from him.

Sam and his friends studied at the seminary in the morning and at AUC in the afternoon. The evening was spent in the library. Books became Sam's first love, and he spent countless hours in the seminary's library, poring over theological commentaries and studying philosophy, psychology, sociology, church history, historical and Biblical theology and church management.

Occasionally, as time allowed, Sam would attend the Cairo branch of the Society for the Salvation of Souls and accepted invitations to preach in Cairo's churches. But for the most part he immersed himself totally in his studies and the extra- curricular reading he set himself.

In those days, books were hard to obtain in Egypt. However, under the guidance of the Rev. Willis A. McGill, an American missionary and seminary professor, Sam purchased books from the United States and England through catalogues McGill acquired for the students. Sam was hooked. From that time on he devoted a certain portion of his monthly income to establishing his own personal library encouraged by McGill. The other young seminarians quickly followed his example. In time he built up a library numbering more than 6,000 volumes, covering all the major disciplines.

The Rev. McGill also instructed Sam in New Testament exegesis and studies in the life of Christ. He taught Sam to think critically about issues, and while Sam was by nature critical, especially with reference to his local community in Tahta, McGill helped Sam to think critically in more positive ways.

McGill's teaching on the life of Christ profoundly affected young Sam and deeply influenced his understanding of Jesus's own ministry, life and calling. It would be a model for the young Sam in later years.

It was while studying at the seminary and university that Sam learned to think across disciplines. He started relating Christianity to psychology, sociology and the social sciences, and he began to reflect theologically on Christian lifestyles. He studied anthropology and local customs in an attempt to understand the relationship between Christian belief and Egyptian culture, particularly certain customs and habits that conditioned the thinking of uneducated Egyptians, often making them fear changes that he saw were absolutely necessary if they were to move forward with their lives, especially in the villages.

Sam's theological mentors included Dr. Labib Mishriqi, under whom he learned hermeneutics and pastoral theology, and Dr. Tawfiq Salih. Dr. Mishriqi was at that time a great leader of the Synod of the Nile, and later became a strong supporter and advocate of young Sam's ministry. Sam also came under the influence of another American Presbyterian missionary, Dr. Earl E. Elder, who taught church history and gave his students in-depth perspectives into Western thinking and the history of the church.

Another teacher who had a profound influence on Sam's life was Dr. Amir Boktor, who taught psychology at AUC. Study at the American University was expensive, but Sam obtained a scholarship from the university to study under Dr. Boktor through the good graces of John S. Badeau, the university president.

Badeau was an ordained Presbyterian minister who later became United States ambassador to Egypt during the last days of President Nasser.

It was in Boktor's psychology classes that Sam began to think seriously about many of the behavioural practices going on in Egyptian society that were culturally conditioned and posed an obstacle to progress and development. Sam began to think through the issues both psychologically and theologically, and to frame a response in his mind to the changes he saw were absolutely necessary for a new and emerging society. His studies at AUC also afforded him a chance to improve his English. Bilingualism was vital to Sam's future.

He found that his fellow-students spoke English almost flawlessly, while he himself still lagged behind. He worked hard reading everything he could in English and conversing only in English while at the university.

Another influential figure whom Sam greatly admired was the dean of the seminary, Rev. Dr. Gabriel Rizkallah, who over the course of time became like a father to him. It was Rizkallah who later ordained Sam to the ministry and who officiated at Sam's wedding.

Sam made many deep and lasting friendships at the seminary. His colleagues all became pastors. One of his closest friends and a special confidant, Dr. Fayez Faris, later accepted the pastorship of the Second Evangelical Church in Minia, Middle Egypt, establishing it as one of the most vital spiritual centres of Christian growth in Upper Egypt.

Among his other close personal friends were the Rev. Dr. Menis Abdel-Noor and Dr Swailem Sidhom. Menis Abdel-Noor, a great preacher and Bible study leader, shared in CEOSS's literature work in the Sixties and later became pastor of the largest Evangelical Church in the Middle East; Swailem Sidhom spent some years in southern Sudan as the Egyptian Evangelical Church's first missionary, then went to the United States to complete his studies and later became Professor of Social Sciences at the University of Illinois.

Sam also made friends with Dr. Fahim Aziz, a great theological scholar who later obtained his doctorate from Edinburgh University in Scotland and returned to teach at the seminary in Cairo. Fahim and Sam were the two acknowledged readers of the class, and regularly woke each other up at 4 a.m. to read in the library before breakfast. After breakfast they would return to the library and read through the day and late into the night. Sam's other close friend was the Rev. Adib Habib, whose special gift in music quickly got him appointed chapel organist. He later became pastor of the Evangelical Church in Fayoum.

Sam's father's library had been rich in biblical study materials, and he had subscribed to a number of biblical journals. This had stimulated much of Sam's early thinking, but it had its limitations. Now, with the seminary and university libraries at his disposal, Sam was able to throw himself totally into reading theology and liberal arts, broadening his education at every turn.

It was during this period that Sam also wrote and published his first two books, primarily to help young people. The first was on *Prayer* (now in its seventh edition), and the second on *How to Face Temptation* (now in its sixth edition).

The book on Prayer was amended in later editions as Sam's thinking matured. One particular issue on which he challenged conventional thinking was the matter of women covering their heads to pray. In the early editions he had not mentioned the issue, because he had not thought about the cultural context surrounding head coverings for women. In later editions, following his seminary and AUC training, he amended the book to argue that head coverings were not necessary. His studies in theology and culture had convinced him that women's head coverings were not a primary issue of faith but a matter of culture, and could be dispensed with without damage to the central core of Christian truth.

In his second book, on *How To Face Temptation*, Sam expounded some daring if not entirely radical views on human sexuality that got him denounced from some pulpits. While he was not exactly branded a heretic, his thoughts and writings were considered highly inappropriate at that time.

The topic of masturbation, for example, was considered highly taboo as a subject of conversation among conservative Christians, and the church had long declared it a sin that caused physical and mental disorders.

Sam, however, concluded from his studies in both psychology and theology that masturbation was not wrong or scientifically harmful as the church said, and that the church's stance only caused needless suffering for young people facing puberty and the growing awareness of their own sexuality. It created in them a false sense of guilt.

Writing about this in the Forties was a courageous and difficult thing to do, but Sam acted out of conscience and his own study of both Scripture and psychology. He felt the issue had to be confronted directly, as a whole new generation of young Egyptians were growing up in need of understanding about the subject. The topic could no longer be swept under the rug. Both books were at first published privately with Sam's father putting up the money and Sam assisting in the type-setting to minimize costs.

More than 1,000 copies of the books were printed and sold out within a month. Several more editions appeared over the years, resulting in the sale of tens of thousands of books.

In May 1950 Sam graduated from the seminary with a Bachelor's Degree in Theology. Two years later, while beginning to focus his thinking on the enormous problems facing his country, he received his B.A. in Social Sciences from the American University.

Sam's formal education now drew to a close. His academic training had been rigorous. He had studied under some of the most renowned names in the Egyptian church. He had learned much and, while he had not yet been tested in the real world, his time spent in study at the seminary and university had challenged him at many different levels. It had helped him see the unity of knowledge, the relationship between science and religion, and how he was able to reflect on what was uniquely Biblical and what was cultural. Above all, it enabled him to see the need for the church to be more deeply involved in society. The churches in Egypt, particularly the Coptic Orthodox Church and the Evangelical Church, were very inward-looking and pietistic. There was little evangelistic zeal and almost no social outreach to the poorest in Egyptian society. The old habit of benevolent giving by almost everybody still prevailed, but most churches would give only to the poor in their own congregations.

To withdraw from society, as the Egyptian churches were effectively doing, was to evade their responsibility to the broader community. Sam could no longer condone that. It was this that touched Sam's soul the most and ignited the flame in his imagination.

Sam served notice to anyone who would listen that change was in the air. A new chapter was about to be written not only in his own personal life but in the life of the Christian churches in Egypt. He was about to take a bold step forward and go where no one had gone before.

Chapter 2

A Vision Unfolds

In April 1950, just prior to graduating from seminary, Sam was offered his first job. He had been assigned by the Synod to work in one of the Evangelical churches in the province of Suhag, but after prayerful consideration he turned the offer down. Instead he asked for a one-year study leave without salary. It was a courageous act, as he was going against all the tradition of the Evangelical Church, which viewed seminary graduates as prime candidates for needy churches around the country. Sam did not yet know what he wanted to do, but he had not felt a particular call to the pastoral ministry, and he wanted to wait on God for a more decisive understanding of his future direction.

Sam had spent his early years in public preaching. Now he had a seminary training and had put in thousands of hours of private reading to improve himself. He had steeped himself in literature and learning way beyond ninety-nine percent of his people, and in a sense he now felt isolated. But he saw in literature an important medium for education and communication of the gospel, and he had begun to catch a glimpse of how important literature work could be as a valid arm of the church's ministry to reach Egypt's millions. He felt it deserved better treatment than it was getting, and warranted full-time workers. However, the general thinking of the church at that time was quite opposed to the idea.

The pastorate was considered the highest and noblest calling for a trained seminary graduate, and Sam's decision not to heed what they felt was his call provoked a lot of heated discussion and some concern among his peers and professors. But Sam had not felt the call to the pastorate and he would not yield to public pressure on the matter.

He saw in literature work, however, an opportunity for Christians in the churches, many of whom were spiritually immature, to grow in their faith. At another level, he saw a larger and more overwhelming need. He began to view with deep concern the vast illiteracy of millions of Egypt's rural poor men, women and children who could not read or write even their own names.

Sam also saw that the nation's church leaders were not giving the priority to literature work that he saw was necessary, indeed essential, if the church was to grow numerically and spiritually in the years ahead, and the people be generally helped in the totality of their lives. Literacy would enable people to participate in plans to improve their health, nutrition, living conditions, economic opportunities and general cultural awareness.

Illiteracy, on the other hand, was a no-win situation for both the church and the people. If people outside the church could not read or write they would quite possibly remain ignorant all their lives, and they would never be able to read the Bible for themselves. No one else was educating them, and if the churches did not teach them to read they would remain illiterate and stay victims of their own oppressive circumstances.

Help came from an entirely unexpected quarter. A missionary with the United Presbyterian Church of North America in the person of Dr. Davida M. Finney was looking for someone to assist her in setting up church libraries and preparing materials for literacy work. This was a project that was still very much in the experimental stage in Egypt.

Finney was the Egyptian-born daughter of American Presbyterian missionaries, and an only child. She grew up speaking perfect Arabic and was very popular with the church and much loved by the Egyptian people. For her part, she loved Egypt and its people and was considered by many to be a visionary with extraordinary discernment into Egypt's problems. Yet because of her stand on literacy and literature for Egypt's masses she found little respect from some of her American missionary colleagues. Her vision for Egypt's poor was not on their agenda of concerns. Davida was responsible for the joint Church/Mission Literature Committee of the Synod of the Nile and the Presbyterian Mission, with headquarters in Cairo. Her job afforded her the unique opportunity to travel around Egypt, not only visiting the churches and developing their libraries but also observing the distressing living conditions of millions of Egypt's rural poor, most of whom could not read or write.

On the committee were four of Egypt's top Christian leaders

from the Evangelical Church; Dr. Ibrahim Sa'id, Dr. Labib Mishriqi, Dr. Tawfiq Salih and Dr. Boutros Abdel-Malik as well as a number of Western missionaries, including Davida herself.

Davida's top priority was setting up libraries in churches. A main library had been established in the American Mission building in Ezbekieh, downtown Cairo, and she had set up other libraries in churches around the country. Davida's desire was to give people access to Christian books written in simple Arabic, and to tie this into a new literacy programme that she had initiated.

Davida had begun in 1948, with Frank C. Laubach, the American pioneer of worldwide literacy, to teach illiterates in a massive literacy campaign across the country. She had, to date, put some five years of disciplined hard work into the programme, but it had failed. Discouraged, she sought to refocus her efforts in one area alone, but she needed help. She knew she could not do it alone and risk failure again. If she failed, the programme would be terminated.

A friend of Sam's told Davida that he was about to graduate from seminary and might be a suitable candidate for the job. He pointed out that Sam had already published two excellent Christian books that were selling well among young people. Both books had been given to Davida by the Rev. Labib Kaldas, pastor of the Palais Evangelical Church in Alexandria and a personal friend of Sam's. Davida read the books and was at once impressed by the author's faith and commitment. On Labib's recommendation she interviewed Sam. She listened to his concerns and felt an immediate affinity with his thinking. Without even considering other candidates, she hired Sam on the spot.

Her love for Egypt and its people reflected Sam's, and what she needed was a totally dedicated, educated and native-born Egyptian Christian helper capable of collaborating with her. In Sam she saw not only the person she was looking for but also the way forward. By choosing the right Egyptian assistant, she felt confident of the complete success of the programme.

In accepting this position Sam was venturing, for the first time, into the real world of ordinary people, the everyday life of millions of Egyptians outside the sheltered world of seminary and the stimulus of intellectual friends and university life. It also brought him into greater contact with the Christian community in Cairo.

His radical views on women in the church were also being put to the test. The irony of the situation was not lost on him. His first boss was a woman, an American no less, with deep roots in Egyptian soil and culture, its people and heritage.

In April 1950, then, Sam began working with Davida in the Literature Department, from an office near the library in the American Mission building. It was an auspicious beginning. Sam's work involved selecting and writing suitable materials for printing, while helping this energetic woman run the main library in Cairo as well as set up branches in churches all over the country. As there were just the two of them working together, the job afforded Sam a lot of flexibility, and allowed him to maintain his rigorous programme of studies at the American University in Cairo. His salary in those days was the equivalent of about US$50 dollars a month, not much, but he was able to survive and get by.

By the time of his graduation from AUC in 1952, Sam was becoming more and more convinced of the possibilities of the Literature Department of the church. His mind now began to focus on the possibility of literature and literacy education working together to benefit Egypt's poor in a unique new way.

He made up his mind then and there that this was going to be the immediate focus of his future ministry, and immediately set about making new plans. For a start, he returned to AUC for one more year and took a degree course in journalism to help him in his writing and literature work while he continued working for Davida.

In November 1952 he was ordained by the Evangelical Church of Egypt and the Synod of the Nile for Special Services in Literature, and was immediately appointed General Secretary for Christian Literature for Egypt and the Sudan. His ordination took place at the Evangelical Church in Ezbekiya, Cairo, and was performed by the Rev. Dr. Gabriel Rizkallah, the man who was later to officiate at his marriage.

Sam was the first Egyptian in the church's history ever to be ordained and appointed to do literature work, and as he began to focus on literacy work he met with opposition from colleagues in both the Orthodox and Protestant churches for doing something they did not consider a religious work. Some of his friends even stopped supporting him in spirit. Sam was unmoved by their rejection and simply resolved to work even harder. He had no doubts about the necessity of his work.

Shortly after this, Sam's career took another turn which at first he did not entirely welcome. It involved literacy work in an Egyptian village community. The invitation came from Davida Finney herself.

The literacy programme begun by Davida appealed enormously to Sam. It used the Laubach method, a word/picture method of teaching people to read and write designed for use in the Third World. Egypt was one of the first countries involved in this new approach to literacy, which was being introduced into some 50 countries around the world. It seemed to work well in most places and continued until the 1960s, when a new method was introduced by UNESCO experts. But so far it had not done well in Egypt.

Working with Dr. Hilana Mikhail, an Egyptian colleague who later received an honourary doctorate for her work, and Marjorie Dye, an American Presbyterian missionary who later worked loyally for CEOSS, showing great adaptability and love for the Egyptian people until her retirement in 1958, Davida had expanded the literacy programme over all the country. Because it was spread too thin, however, the programme had failed. Results from several years of work with the programme were consistently disappointing. There were many reasons for the failure. Local leaders had not been well trained, and most of them were not convinced of the need or importance of literacy for their people.

Davida was desperate for the programme to succeed, but she needed to rethink her strategy. The failure of the programme to date would have made a lesser person throw in the towel and give up. Not so Davida. She was a woman of profound Christian character, conviction and perseverance; and with the future hopes of literacy for millions of Egyptians hanging on her decision, she was not about to do anything to fail or disappoint them.

In those days Laubach was working with a department of the National Council of Churches of Christ in the U.S. called the World Literacy and Christian Literature Committee, known as 'Lit-Lit'. Its purpose was to promote literacy and literature around the world.

In 1952 'Lit-Lit' gave Davida just one more year to pull it all together and make a success of the literacy programme in Egypt, or else they would drop it entirely and all funding would cease. Faced with this ultimatum, she decided that rather than trying to make the programme work all across Egypt and overextend herself, she would focus a literacy campaign in one small community only.

The plan would be to discover people's actual motives for learning to read and write, conduct experiments to test out different teaching methods and materials and then move the whole project into high gear.

Davida Finney reached out to Sam for help. He was the perfect fit for the programme, and she saw in him and the team she had pulled together a real possibility for its revival and success. She approached him with an offer. Would Sam, only 22 and untested, move to a single village and try again to make the literacy programme work? Sam was far from enthusiastic, but he agreed.

Anticipating Sam's acceptance, Davida had already written to Evangelical churches all over the country asking pastors whether their communities would like to host this literacy experiment. Only one had replied. In the sovereignty of God, the person who wrote in was none other than the Rev. Menis Abdel-Noor, a personal friend of Sam's from their seminary days who now pastored the Evangelical Church in Nazlit Herz, a village in the Middle Egyptian province of Minia. Without knowing of Sam's involvement and concern he answered the call and took up the challenge.

While Sam was not yet truly convinced of the value of the literacy programme and had no real desire to go and live in a village community, he could not really say no. Menis was after all his friend, and he had no wish to let him down. But the thought of village life, the dirt, the filth, of being surrounded by unhealthy people and the lack of home comforts, was more than he could bear to think of.

Furthermore, he was already sold on literature work, which he wanted to continue in Cairo and in Egypt's larger city churches. So why give it all up for a single literacy programme in a village, with little hope of success or a future that he could see for himself? The reasons for going finally boiled down to supporting his old friend Menis, who clearly saw the need for a literacy programme among his own people. Also, Davida was pushing him very hard.

Sam had only spent two short periods of time in village communities before this, during summer breaks from seminary. On these occasions he had been somewhat sheltered from real village life, staying close to the church and mingling very little with the local people. Furthermore, the bulk of his experience had been in cities like Tahta and Cairo, and he had never learned to get down and dirty with ordinary people.

He was about to learn. After much prayer and meditation, the way forward seemed clear. He would go, even though he believed it was not in any way a career move. He sensed, however, that this might be the call of God on his life at this moment in time, and he couldn't and wouldn't ignore it. Perhaps, who could tell, it might lead to something more?

Deep down he knew that if he was going to help his people in any measurable way, sooner or later he would have to leave the security of his office and the comparative comfort of life in Cairo. In his heart Sam knew it was time to leave. The rural areas around Minia beckoned. And so Sam packed his few belongings, said farewell to family and friends, and took off in the "Lit-Lit" car to Nazlit Herz.

His move to rural Egypt proved radically life-changing. When he arrived in the village Sam experienced a moment of profound culture shock, the like of which he had never experienced before. His eyes were suddenly opened and for the first time he saw the people in their need and poverty: it hit him like a ton of bricks.

From the first moment he saw them he was overcome with a compassion for the people in their wretched situation such as he had never felt before. He had stepped back in time, centuries it seemed, to a world he hardly knew. Yet these people lived right on his doorstep.

He knew they had always been there, but their presence had never truly entered his consciousness till now. Sam's life had been essentially urban, middle-class and intellectual. Now he was being reminded of how the other half or more accurately eighty percent of the country lived: in villages where hygiene was virtually non-existent, water was contaminated and diseases were endemic, and where men, women and children were crammed into tiny mud and mortar houses, sometimes six or more to a room, while working long hours for subsistence wages.

Sam saw, for the first time, the vast masses of illiterate and impoverished people, and realized that literacy would not only enable them to read and study the Word of God for themselves but also help them to make improvements in all aspects of their lives. He decided then and there that serving them would be his first calling.

Sam's real education had now only just begun. The lessons he would learn here would shape both his future ministry and the rest of his life. In moving to the village he had taken the first and biggest step of faith in his life. God had lessons to teach Sam, lessons that could only be learned in the village experiences of life, far from the excitement of the cities, sophisticated urban crowds and comfortable middle-class churches. This gifted young man would now learn what it meant to be a servant for his Lord: to wash feet rather than pontificate from pulpits six feet above contradiction.

The literacy team of five comprised Sam, Davida Finney, the American missionary Marjorie Dye, Hilana Mikhail and Menis, the pastor of the local church. Working together they began a new campaign of literacy in Egypt. On their success or failure hung the future chances of millions of Egypt's poor to learn to read and write.

Young Sam moved in with the pastor and his wife. They gave him a room from where he began his work – in reality the start of a new life. He began visiting the people in their homes. They would greet him with smiles, happy to see the 'pastor', but Sam saw behind the smiles to the problems they faced in their lives. As he sat with the people and listened to their stories of hope and despair, he slowly began to gain their confidence.

The village of Herz consisted of a thousand people, all of them farmers and ninety percent of them Christians. As often in communities in rural Egypt, there was one rich family: the mayor and his relatives. The rest of the people lived in varying degrees of poverty. As a community, they would go out in the morning to labour in their fields of wheat and cotton and return tired and worn out in the evening, seven days a week.

He visited the farmers, asking hundreds of questions and learning why they farmed they way they did, and how much of what they did traced directly back to the traditions and customs of ancient Egypt. Sam was humbled by what he saw and experienced.

Along with deep superstitions and traditions that had grown up over centuries and dominated people's lives, often to their detriment, the River Nile held within its meandering grasp the lives of millions.

For example water, the life-blood of Egypt, could now be pumped up from wells in the ground bringing cleaner and fresher water for drinking and the purposes of irrigation, yet the people clung to the mystique of water coming directly from the Nile, as though their lives depended on it.

Slowly, ever so slowly, Sam learned that according to an old superstition going back to ancient Egypt, the water of the Nile has fertility properties, and women would not give birth to children if they ever stopped drinking it. So the villagers continued to take their drinking water from the Nile, despite the fact that its polluted waters brought crippling diseases and sometimes death if drunk unboiled. Dysentery, together with malnutrition, kept the average lifespan of a villager to around 40 years. A person was considered very old to have made it to 50.

There were other traditions the people practised which mingled ancient superstition with Christian rites. One of these surrounded death. It was thought that after death a person's spirit, while it had left the body, remained in the room for three days, and a ceremony had to be performed to dismiss it. Over the course of time the Coptic Orthodox Church had incorporated this ceremony into its liturgy, and offered a special ritual for the dead with incense, even though the church did not officially believe that the spirit stayed in the room. It simply absorbed into its rites ancient practices going back to the time of the Pharaohs.

This mingling of religion and superstition caught Sam off guard. He had no idea such things were being practised. His own background in the Evangelical Church and his entire theological training repudiated such religious syncretism. But Sam learned to listen. God was speaking to Sam through the lives of his people, and Sam was forced to hear.

The literacy programme challenged Sam as nothing else had done before. It was demanding from day one. He and the team wrote the first books ever for the people of Nazlet Herz. They learned and wrote by listening to the people and their needs as they journeyed along together. Problems were encountered, mistakes were made, and challenges confronted, but the team adapted. The programme went forward and the experiment in literacy turned out to be a huge success.

The five months the five of them spent in the village of Herz was a completely new learning experience for all of them, overwhelming at times but a total education in itself. Not only did the literacy programme take root and grow, it was so successful that it quickly became worldwide news and was written up in a number of Western newspapers and magazines. *The Reader's Digest* sent its deputy editorial manager from the United States to the village of Herz to write for its millions of readers about the success of the literacy programme, prompting other news media to send their reporters and editors to analyze the programme as well.

The literacy experiment succeeded beyond anyone's wildest imagination. Of the 1,000 village residents, twelve percent became literate within a matter of months, and by July 1953 the number of new literates had doubled to twenty-four percent.

Between 1953 and 1955 the programme expanded to the neighbouring communities of Ezbet Diab and Gaweer, resulting in 400 men and women learning to read and write, and in September 1955 the team initiated a follow-up literacy programme, with a view to training local leaders to take over.

Buoyed by the success of the programme, Sam inaugurated, a year later, a new magazine called Risalet El Noor (Message of Light), a monthly development magazine targeted especially at new literates who wanted and needed to maintain their literacy standards. This proved a personal triumph for Sam, and the beginning of the fulfilment of his dreams for his people.

In the years that followed, the magazine expanded to provide new literates with easy-to-read articles on health, agriculture, mother and child care, and problem-solving in family relationships. The magazine even invited dialogue with the Governor of Minia on a number of pressing social issues. Today, under its current editorial team, the magazine sells more than 65,000 copies a year.

For Sam, the immediate lessons he learned about village life gave him a broader perspective and deeper awareness of other needs of his people that he had never seen before. It was not only their need to read and write that Sam saw, but also the villagers' needs for clean water, hygiene, agricultural development, tools, different types of farming and overall rural development. This kind of knowledge could dramatically change their lives, offering them better standards of living and increasing productivity on a scale they could so far only dream about. Such development could radically change and improve not only their own lives but those of their children and generations to follow.

The poverty and backwardness of Christian and Muslim alike challenged him to the very depth of his being. God had opened

Sam's eyes to the vast array of his people's needs – needs that he would now attempt to address over the course of a lifetime of service.

As he looks back to the beginning of his ministry in that small, seemingly irrelevant village, Sam can see the hand of God working in his life through a single, committed woman: Davida Finney. Her commitment to him had not only changed his life and given him direction for his ministry; it forever affected how he would view women and the place they would have in any ministry God might have for his future.

So impressed was she by the success of the literacy programme that Davida extended her time in Egypt three years beyond the stipulated retirement age in order to promote it. She finally left Egypt in her 68th year and returned to the United States, where she died.

Though single and alone, she was never lonely. Her life left an indelible imprint on the lives of thousands of Egyptians who, through her efforts, learned to read and write. Her most profound influence, though, had been on the mind and heart of young Samuel Habib. When she died many mourned Davida Finney's passing, but none more so than Samuel Habib.

Young Sam's journey had just begun. He had taken his first tentative steps in faith. More steps would follow. The next stage in his journey would take him to America.

For now, though, he could reflect on the lessons learned in that small village in the province of Minia in Middle Egypt and be thankful.

The success of the literacy programme was now known world-wide and later prompted other churches and organizations in Egypt, including Muslim groups, to copy what they had done. Some used the Lit-Lit team's ideas on literacy in their own programmes; others used their own materials. Sam and the others assisted them in any way they could. There was no copyright on truth. Sam wanted to establish literacy as a birthright for all Egyptians and not merely an option.

Samuel Habib returned to Cairo a changed man. The next ten years would be the toughest in his life, years of intense and very real struggle. They would make him or break him. But young Samuel Habib was made of stern stuff. He was in it for the long haul. Only God knew the way ahead. Sam would follow even though the way might at times seem unclear, frustrated by human obstacles and fraught with dangers. But he was committed to his people and to the God who saw not only a sparrow fall to the ground, but every living soul that needed a helping hand along the Nile.

Chapter 3

Moving Out

A STEP OF FAITH

Sam stood awkwardly but determinedly on the stage in front of his all-American audience of several hundred men and women. A few moments earlier he had been given his subject: 'What you like and don't like about America'. There was no advance warning, no time think, plan or make notes. He just had to speak. He had only been in the country four months and had been invited, along with a number of other foreigners, to offer an American audience their impressions of the United States. Bold, unafraid, and with complete confidence, Sam spoke.

It was 1954, and at the age of 26 Sam was making his first trip outside of his native Egypt. His first stop: the United States. He had been offered a scholarship by the National Council of Churches of Christ and its committee on World Literacy and Christian Literature to study at Syracuse University in upstate New York. It was to be the beginning of a lifetime of international travel that would focus his efforts on helping Egypt's teeming masses.

He arrived in the U.S. eager to learn all he could. For the next eighteen months, until 1955, he would focus his efforts on journalism and obtain a Master's degree. This period also marked a renewal of his vision for literacy and literature programmes for the poor and marginalized among Egypt's men, women and children.

In the United States Sam planned to use his time to broaden his horizons and thinking in every way he could. He would leave no stone unturned in his search for knowledge, knowledge that would help him move the Christian church in Egypt forward.

His studies at the university would be only a part of his total education. Sam planned to throw himself into studying the life and ministries of the Presbyterian Church and the activities of the

National Council of Churches, observing their programmes first
hand and absorbing ideas that he could implement back in Egypt.

He spent the summers of 1954 and 1955 visiting churches
throughout the country, meeting pastors and young people and
evaluating youth programmes.

In 1954 he attended the Second World Assembly of the World
Council of Churches in Evanston, Illinois, as a press delegate
covering the news for the religious press of Egypt. This was Sam's
first contact with world church leaders and the vital issues confronting the church universal, and he became intoxicated in the heady
atmosphere. Such global gatherings had always seemed so distant
and somehow unreal to him, yet now he was there listening to the
church's challenges and taking copious notes to ponder and reflect
upon later.

As a member of the press corps, Sam had access to position papers
from all the various committees discussing the important theological issues of the day. Sam, of course, voraciously read all he could,
studying these papers in depth and catching glimpses here and there
of ideas he could translate into the Egyptian context. Because of his
status as a journalist he was permitted to go anywhere, attend any
meeting, ask any question and interview any church leader. This
gave him unprecedented exposure to people he would never have
met in the normal course of his life, and certainly would never have
rubbed shoulders with in Egypt. All at once he was in touch with
the world church.

He observed the church leaders with a measure of curiosity and
awe. To actually be in touch with these men and women at this
young age gave him deeper insights into the universal church and
the major issues it faced, and widened the horizons of his thinking
beyond the parochial and very limited stage he was used to.

Racism and apartheid and the church's social responsibility were
beginning to emerge as major themes of deliberation. The new
word for the day was 'ecumenical'. The church was now being
presented as one big brotherhood united under its Lord, prepared
to step forth and do battle with the powers of darkness.

In Egypt, Sam had been involved in some activities of the
Near East Christian Council, a missionary group made up of
Middle East denominational leaders. Its concerns were strictly
local and did not reflect the broader global issues he was now
confronting.

Because he had already been involved in missionary activities in Egypt and had known and worked with a number of missionaries, and had actually worked for one in the person of Davida Finney, he had touched the fringe of the international Christian community. Now he desperately wanted not only to broaden his thinking through study but also to observe and learn all he could about the life of the church in the United States, and to capture the essence of American life in general.

Following the conclusion of the WCC Assembly, Sam travelled to other ecumenical conferences around the United States, including a number of youth conferences associated with the Presbyterian Church (U.S.A.). As he travelled the U.S. and studied, he knew that his year's stay would not be nearly long enough. He needed more time to explore the life of the church and then digest and evaluate his overall American experience.

After considerable discussion with his advisors it was agreed that he would stay an extra six months, spending the summers doing additional studies and travelling the country, absorbing all he could of American church life before returning to Egypt.

At Syracuse University Sam encountered the rich pluralism that distinguishes so much of the intellectual climate of America. Among other people, he met and made friends with an Indian who was on the same scholarship programme as himself. Together they discussed the implications of being a minority religion in their respective countries.

Sam also entered into the multifarious activities of student campus life with complete abandon. At times it overwhelmed him. The life of a student at an Egyptian university could not compare with the wide-ranging experiences he was now encountering on an American campus. The freedom was exhilarating.

An opportunity to address an all-American audience on his likes and dislikes about American life both intrigued and fascinated Sam. His audience that day was a typical mix of Americans, and the purpose of his speech, he discovered later, was to help Americans understand what it was foreigners liked and disliked about their country.

As the first of several speakers that day, he told his audience that he was deeply moved by the American ideas of freedom and progress and he was greatly impressed by the country's structures, organization, administration and progress in technology.

Then, typical of himself, Sam went on to criticize the way
children were raised in the United States. The freedoms teenagers
were given were more than they could handle, he said, and their
wild ways troubled him. Such things had not been his experience,
he told them, growing up in Egypt, where his father was very much
head of the house and his views were meant to be respected. Sam
spoke for fifteen minutes and then sat down. The audience rose to
its feet and applauded him. Sam was deeply moved by this open
display of warmth. It is not something he would have experienced
in Egypt.

Coming from the hot climate of the Middle East, Sam encountered snow for the first time and revelled in it with his Indian
colleague. It was not unusual for them to go out and play in the
snow in temperatures that reached forty degrees below zero. They
would return to their rooms completely covered in the white stuff,
and later pay the price in stiff hands and cold feet. But they would
take the experience back to their countries and remember the
United States in all its rich diversity including the weather.

Sam made many new friendships during his eighteen months in
the United States. He was constantly invited into American homes
to enjoy American hospitality, and he was asked at least twice a
month to speak to church groups and youth clubs about the church
In Egypt.

Sam planned to finish his coursework in one year and use the
summer for more visitation and field experience. His advisor said
it couldn't be done, but Sam persevered and finished on schedule.
He graduated with his journalism courses complete in May 1955.
These included courses on magazine production, article writing and
news writing which proved of great value back in Egypt. His
imagination was also captured by a course in writing for new
literates under the title 'Literacy Journalism', taught by Bob
Laubach, the son of Frank C. Laubach.

Later he was introduced to Frank Laubach himself, whose
literacy methodology he had been using in the rural villages of
Egypt.

It was a meeting of the minds, and through their conversation
Sam recognized Laubach's deep concern for the world's millions
caught in the trap of ignorance and illiteracy, and his commitment
to the Lit-Lit programme as a way for the church to engage in the
task of reaching out to illiterates.

Sam's educational experiences in the United States also confirmed and built on his experiences at the American University in Cairo. The 'can do' attitudes of Americans greatly impressed him. He saw how Americans got things done, how change was possible in communities, and how people modified their ideas quickly if they saw a better way to do things.

Sam's time in America also helped him to stand firm on some of the beliefs and ideas that he had developed in Egypt, especially with reference to the place and role of women in the church and society. The feminist movement had not yet broken open in America, but the freedom in general of women in American church life, even in the 1950s, far exceeded anything in Egypt. He saw women taking leadership roles in the church and in life which only confirmed his own beliefs about the roles he wanted to see women play in Egyptian society and the Egyptian church.

During his breaks from university, Sam visited a large number of Protestant churches doing mission work in the United States. He was greatly impressed by what he saw. Their aggressiveness and determination without belligerence were qualities he greatly admired.

The broad openness of the church and its place as the centre of community life, the vitality of its youth clubs, the democratic approach to church politics, and the involvement of the elders and lay leaders of the church with the pastor also profoundly touched him. He saw how the older generation respected the ideas of younger people and their need to be heard and express themselves. He recalled how differently young people in Egypt were sometimes treated by the churches and their leaders. In the Egypt of the 1950s, young people were not taken very seriously. They were meant to be seen and not heard. They were also required to dress conservatively and appear very formal. In America he saw young people behaving informally in dress and speech, and he found this compelling. It made life simpler and helped people relate to each other more easily.

He saw how church and state reflected the same democratic principles in the way each functioned, and this deeply impressed young Sam. He found no area of life or concern that could not be addressed in the context of the church. This made Sam bolder in his talks to American young people, especially with regard to matters of sexuality. American churches were open to sermons and frank discussions about human sexuality in ways they were not in Egypt.

That was but one of many changes Sam planned to make on his return. He was determined that in one way or another he would take the lead in speaking more openly about such matters and not sweeping them under the rug.

The modern world, with its good and bad influences, was about to impact his country; serious issues would need to be addressed, and questions would need answering in the light of Scripture as the cultural landscape of Egypt began to change.

Sam knew that serious discussions and dialogue were needed on issues of human sexuality and relationships. The practice of female circumcision, for example, which was still performed on most young Egyptian girls by Christians and Muslims alike, would have to be addressed and stopped. The equally humiliating and age-old custom of having a midwife penetrate a bride's vagina on her wedding night, to see if she was still a virgin, also had to be addressed and ended.

Sam also began to recognize the trauma of early marriage for Egyptian girls, sometimes as young as ten, usually resulting in pregnancy before they became teenagers. He knew that by having babies at such an early age girls completely inhibited their future lives, with several growing children to care for. They lost their youthful innocence, became burdened with cares beyond their years, remained illiterate and often died young.

The thought of all this deeply troubled and angered young Sam Habib. He began to yearn for the time he could return to his native Egypt and boldly speak out against these ancient and unjustified practices, liberating women from the bondage of ancient customs and habits and bringing them into real freedom. His heart ached for the people of rural Egypt in their poverty, illiteracy and ignorance.

Another thing that impressed Sam in the United States was the incredible freedom Americans enjoyed to worship God, and their impressive record on human rights, including the role of women in the community and in the church and the freedom teenagers had to control their own lives and destinies.

In fact it was the issue of freedom above all else that captured his imagination and held his attention. The guarantee of freedoms in the American Constitution profoundly moved him. Back home,

Egypt in the 1950s was experiencing internal revolution. King Farouk had been deposed; Gamal Abdel-Nasser, a military man, had come to power; and in 1956 British occupation forces would finally leave the country. Sam now yearned for the same kinds of freedom for himself and his own people as Americans enjoyed.

His eighteen months in the U.S. soon came to an end. In the fall of 1955, after concluding his studies and graduating, Sam packed his bags and flew back to Egypt fresh with new ideas he wanted to implement, and a clearer vision of what could be done in the service of his people and through the church.

On at least one issue he was absolutely sure: he did not want to import American culture into Egyptian society or the church. The American Presbyterians who founded what was now the Evangelical Church in Egypt had maintained in many respects a very western-style institution. But what Sam wanted to do was to utilize only the best of what he had learned in the United States and apply it in the context of the Egyptian church and people.

Sam feared that the encroachments of Western culture would come soon enough, with the burgeoning worldwide entertainment and communications industry, and he did not want to be part of that. What Sam wanted to do, within the framework of Egyptian society, was to improve the conditions of local communities and tackle the growing problems of poverty in the cities and country-side, particularly the latter.

Sam had his agenda. He wanted to see changes first within the church and then throughout society. He wanted to see age-old customs and practices that were not working discarded. And he wanted to see the church become more open, more vital spiritually and more relevantly involved in the community.

His return to Egypt, however, did not automatically bring changes in his life and opinions, or instant acceptance of his views. Nothing, he knew, would be achieved in a hurry. Besides, he needed to pause and consider in more detail exactly what needed to be done before leaping in to try to bring about radical changes. Caution and discretion were called for, not reckless abandonment of tradition or of the way things had been done in the past.

The churches of Egypt were not suddenly going to change their minds about the role of the pastor or the position of women in the church just because Sam Habib had been exposed to new ideas in the West. What he would do was to begin a movement towards change.

None of the denominations believed in adult literacy work. The primary task of the preacher, as they saw it, was to expound the Word of God to the people. The conditions in which people lived were secondary, even irrelevant to the traditional role of a pastor.

He had a hard time, however, explaining his vision to other Christian friends and to Evangelical church leaders. When he was invited to speak at various meetings and church gatherings, he began arguing for and vigorously defending the task of social service as an intrinsic part of the church's mission and responsibility. Only after seeing some successful experiments carried out did they eventually became convinced.

Sam's desire and intent was to demonstrate the gospel's transcendent message working itself out in practical ways to improve the lot of Egypt's poor and disenfranchised, and he believed the church was the best vehicle to do this, by serving people as Jesus did. But it would be no easy task, and Sam knew he had his work cut out for him.

Many Egyptians returning to their country after travelling abroad for the first time might have experienced a certain culture shock, but Sam did not. He simply stepped back into Egyptian life ready to promote new ideas and his vision of what he saw as the church's future. Sam always had the ability to adapt easily to new circumstances and surroundings, strange food, new customs and new situations.

Unfazed by the chaos and hubbub of Cairo life, or by the painfully unchanging world of rural Egypt, he now had a dream of how things could be done.

Sam returned to work for Davida Finney in the Literacy and Literature Department of the Synod of the Nile. He now moved from Cairo to the smaller city of Minia, to the south, because the work he had started in nearby Herz had proven so successful he was ready now to repeat it at another nearby village. Furthermore, Davida had moved from Cairo and gotten an apartment in the city of Minia where she now lived, calling it the Literacy House. Sam decided, however, to retain his office in Cairo.

Deir Abu Hinnis was a totally Christian community near Minia, on the west bank of the River Nile. Both the Coptic Orthodox Church and the Evangelical Church were strongly represented there. The village was divided into two large communities, separated by a cemetery running down the middle. The village had split into two following a feud between two families half a century earlier, and their differences had never been settled. A new generation had come along, but the tradition of revenge between the families still continued. In fact feuds and vendettas often continued in Egypt for centuries, carried down from one generation to the next. Men carried pistols on their bodies while walking from one community to the other, and no one ever walked through the cemetery at night for fear of being killed.

Sam felt strongly that the church should directly confront the problem head on and no longer avoid it. Rather than just preaching a simple 'come to Jesus' message from the pulpit one Sunday, Sam decided in his next sermon to openly and publicly challenge the age-old feud and revenge syndrome that continued to plague the community.

Sam was determined to relate the gospel to the problems facing the community and not ignore them. As far as he was concerned, to preach the gospel of personal encounter with Jesus Christ in one's life and yet not see it worked out between warring families was to sell short the gospel's truly liberating message. Men were carrying guns right into the church sanctuary, and when they embraced one another in greeting one could feel the weapons on their bodies. Sam condemned the practice of revenge and ordered the guns to be kept at home. He would not allow the Lord's Table to be desecrated by men carrying weapons to it.

Over a period of several months of preaching and courageous personal example, such as walking through the cemetery in defiance of local tradition, Sam began to convince people to think seriously about the issue. Eventually the business of carrying guns to church stopped. It was an auspicious beginning.

Sam was determined to relate the values of the Bible to the community as a whole, not only in the salvation of souls but in the people's whole lifestyle.

The preaching of the gospel, he said, must also address how people should live together, improve their living conditions, fight the harmful superstitions to which they clung and offer a better way of life. Sam wanted desperately to make the Bible real in people's everyday lives, especially in the villages where tradition was particularly strong.

In Deir Abu Hinnis Sam was asked to head the new literacy programme with a staff of fourteen brought in from outside the village. There were as yet no volunteer leaders from within the village. This troubled Sam, as he saw the need for more grass roots involvement, and he set about changing that.

Between 1955 and 1957 he introduced the idea of volunteer leaders drawn from the ranks of the villagers. Sam saw that drawing in staff from outside of the village was not a long-term solution. The question that haunted him was: Who would take over once the full-time staff pulled out? The answer, Sam saw, lay in developing volunteer local leaders rising up from within the ranks of the community itself.

Sam set about teaching and training a new generation of volunteer leaders under the supervision of his own staff, formerly his students. The process was at times painful, with a lot of misunderstandings and disputes along the way. There was considerable trial and error, but in the end the idea caught on.

Over the next twelve months Sam's methods proved enormously successful, and from the experiences and problems he encountered and the solutions he discovered, Sam published two books on leadership training for voluntary social work: *How To Train Local Leaders*, followed by a '*How-To*' manual for staff use. These books followed Sam's first two books on *Prayer* and *How To Face Temptation*, and began to mark him out as a writer who could articulate the issues as well as a leader who could make things happen.

The book and the manual, written in accessible everyday Arabic, proved so successful as a tool for training leaders that they were translated into English and published by the Lit-Lit Department of the NCCC in New York under the title '*Literacy, The Essential Skill: A Handbook for Literacy Workers*', and were used for similar projects in many other developing countries. They were among the first books ever written and produced by a Third World leader on the subject of development, and pioneered the way for a generation that followed.

The educational programme in training local leaders proved so effective that Sam began a comprehensive programme of training for local volunteer leaders in a number of other small communities in the surrounding area. Once trained, they were ready to take up leadership roles in their respective communities.

It was in Deir Abu Hinnis that Sam took another radical stand by bringing two single young Egyptian women onto the staff to live and work among the villagers.

A lot of heated debate and discussion arose in the community, especially from the men. Why did Sam let women live away from their families, in their own apartment? What did their families think of them doing this? Sam took a lot of heat and criticism for his new stand on the role of women, but he held firm to his beliefs. Sam wanted to make it clear what was and was not biblical with respect to social *mores*. He wanted to establish once and for all that women were as important in the development of a community as men, and whether they were married or not was irrelevant. Women were equal to men and would be treated as such, single or married.

When Sam first announced the programme through Egypt's network of Evangelical churches, specifically inviting women to participate, he got only a handful of applications. He screened them and selected two women: Esma Fahmy and Adiba Youssef. Both were a little older than most of the other applicants, and both were single. One came from the large city of Assiut, 75 miles to the south; the other came from the nearby city of Mallawi.

When they began work in the village Sam encountered his second major round of opposition. This time it concerned the age-old code regarding women's clothing. During the summer Sam thought it important that the women be allowed to dress comfortably in short-sleeved blouses and skirts. This immediately outraged the community elders. Church leaders also came to Sam and complained. They argued long and strenuously that the young women should cover their arms and legs if they were going to work in the village.

It was an affront to the village men, they said, to see women so scantily clad. It violated all their traditions. Sam stood firm and held his ground. He gave the leaders a resounding 'no'. He argued that their clothing was appropriate for the heat they had to endure and was not by any standard offensive. Furthermore, he had come to teach the villagers new ways of doing things, not adapt to their old ways of living or accept the status quo. Sam refused to give ground on the issue.

A tremendous uproar broke out in the community and much heated argument flowed back and forth. Endless rounds of meetings were held to discuss the role of women in the community, but eventually Sam won the day. The single women staffers were accepted into the community and began to have a positive impact.

With the appearance of the two single staff women, the village women gradually began to feel more significant and confident in themselves, and started making new plans and changes to their own lives. They slowly became bolder in the demands they made of their menfolk. They wanted more, much more, for their lives.

Many of them learned to read and write. Over the course of time a number of women established their own businesses, and with their new income contributed to the welfare of their children through improved hygiene and health programmes. Gradually, village women began making tremendous strides in their personal and social lives, their self-worth bolstered by the appearance of the single women in the village.

For Sam, however, it was only the beginning. It would be here at Deir Abu Hinnis that the real campaigns for change would be fought, and would be won or lost. What he had experienced with the women staffers was just the tip of the proverbial iceberg.

In this simple village setting Sam set about challenging three centuries-old practices: female circumcision, proving a girl's virginity before marriage, and early marriage. This trio of customs had been the plague of women for centuries, and the formidable barriers erected around them made them appear sacrosanct and immune to change.

Sam was undaunted. What looked like indestructible barriers he was now ready to do battle against. His goal? To totally annihilate these rituals that served no good purpose, and write a new chapter for Egyptian women.

He began his first education campaign against the circumcision of women, a painful and unhygienic practice carried out by both Muslims and Christians. Male circumcision was a deeply-rooted part of Jewish tradition, based on Old Testament teaching, but there was no scriptural basis in any religion, Jewish, Muslim or Christian, for female circumcision.

The origins of the practice were unclear. It was thought to have originated in Africa and been adopted by Arab countries in pre-Islamic times. The truth was that everybody; Christian, Muslim and Jew now practised it, and in Sam's mind everybody was wrong. It had to stop. A stand had to be taken and an end put to this hideous practice that tormented over ninety percent of Egypt's women.

Sam was ready to fire the first salvos against this inhuman practice. He began talking openly about the issue, first to women, then to the village men and then in the churches. He argued that the reason traditionally given for removing a woman's clitoris, and sometimes labia as well was that this would prevent her from sexually misbehaving. However, this had nothing to do with reality. If a woman wanted to be sexually involved with a man, circumcising her would certainly not prevent it from happening.

He was immediately taken to task by the elders of the community, and the debate raged back and forth. How dare a young upstart like Sam Habib even mention this subject, and then go on to talk about it publicly? History, they said, was on the side of the community.

Sam, however, was undeterred. He next launched an all-out campaign to eliminate the practice, focusing on the degrading and dehumanizing effects it had on women as well as the enormous medical problems that flowed from its enforcement. Sam made every possible effort to press for and bring about a complete change of attitude by all the people.

The first thing he did was to put into place a programme of education aimed directly at women, focusing on the dangers of female circumcision and why it would not satisfy the reasons given for its practice. Sam knew that if he first appealed to women, the objects of this awful practice, then in time it would be easier to persuade men that their womenfolk did not need to undergo this ancient ritual of abuse. Everyone would win, especially the women. Sexual pleasure would no longer be the prerogative of men only; women too could enjoy their sexuality if their bodies, especially their sexual organs, were left intact.

The results of the campaign were significant. Slowly the tide began to turn against this age-old practice.

Sam then began to challenge the second major evil that he saw, that of the midwife's role in proving a bride's virginity on her wedding night by penetrating the girl's vagina with her fingers, wiping the blood onto a handkerchief and waving it before the whole community as evidence.

The practice, rooted in Judaism, had been adopted over time by both Muslims and Christians. Sam found this practice particularly distasteful, arguing vehemently that it was dehumanizing, unhygienic, unsafe and just plain wrong, and had to stop. An uproar broke

out in the community. Threats bordered on becoming violent. But
Sam held tenaciously to his convictions.

If such practices could be abolished in the major cities of Cairo
and Alexandria, as was already happening, they could be stopped
in Egypt's villages as well. But talking, Sam knew, was not enough.
He decided to write about these problems, using his magazine for
new literates, *Risalet El Noor* (Message of Light), as a vehicle to
pronounce directly on the issues. Literacy was on the move, and
many women and girls were beginning to read and write for the
first time.

In 1956 he took his most courageous stand to date and wrote his
first editorials condemning both practices, female circumcision and
the wedding-night ritual outright. He mercilessly attacked them as
vile, antiquated, harmful to women's health and culturally back-
ward. The growing women's movement throughout the world and
the rising tide of women's consciousness would not tolerate the
practice of these barbaric customs in the Middle East, he argued.

To try to kill off these dehumanizing practices, Sam sat down
with community leaders and worked out ways to compensate
village midwives whose income and livelihoods depended on them.
Sam developed new projects through which the midwives could
earn money. Many joined his campaign to become Family Planning
and First Aid advisors in their communities. With their basic, if
distorted, knowledge of human anatomy, the midwives were easy
to train and quickly became effective in carrying out their new jobs.

An important start was to persuade religious leaders, both
Muslim and Christian, of the medical and psychological dangers
inherent in these practices, and also to convince them that these
were not religious rites but merely cultural practices handed down
from one generation to the next with no valid reason for observing
them. Sam wanted the community's religious leaders to counsel the
village women and advise them against the practices. He knew it
would carry greater weight if it came from them rather than from
an outsider like himself.

One day, a local Coptic Orthodox priest came to see Sam in his
office in Minia and confronted him with his writings. Sam knew
that whichever way the church went on the subject, that would
decide the community's response. The priest argued that it was not
right for Sam to speak or write on these issues; and that the practices
should best be left alone and the traditions allowed to continue

uninterrupted. Sam then asked the priest point blank which was cleaner and healthier, for girls to read an article and see a photo in a magazine condemning the problem, or for those same girls to endure a midwife's rough handling and see her stand up in public waving a handkerchief smeared with her blood? Which was the more humiliating to endure, which was cleaner? Sam challenged.

The priest listened. A lengthy dialogue followed. A few hours later the priest departed a changed man. Sam had won the first round with an established church leader.

When the next wedding took place in that Orthodox priest's village, the cleric defended the bride's right not to have the midwife come and penetrate her. The bridegroom also said he didn't want the midwife to interfere. Sam said they should tell the midwife not to come, but pay her anyway so that she wouldn't make a fuss in the village and spoil the reputation of the wife-to-be. And that was what was done.

The wedding day was set. It was a Coptic Orthodox wedding and the priest who had visited Sam performed it. The whole village attended. Sam was also invited. Everything proceeded as planned, until the father of the bride got drunk and, realizing that the midwife was not going to come, decided to kill his daughter. In his mind, the midwife's failure to appear meant that his daughter was not pure, not a virgin, a publicly certified virgin and he had to kill her to save his own reputation.

The groom was terrified that the drunken father would carry out his threat. In a bold move Sam stepped in. He told the groom to run and get the midwife. When she arrived, one of the women took her aside and privately told her to cut her finger, put the blood on a handkerchief and wave it in front of the people. The midwife obliged. The handkerchief was waved in public for everyone to see and the matter was settled.

It was a case of deception, but as the father was too drunk to know what had happened, and the midwife had already been paid, no one minded. The important thing was that the girl had not been physically hurt or publicly humiliated. And what transpired at the wedding that day signalled a new direction in the community. It got people thinking seriously about the issues, and it forced them to dig deeper into their traditions and to challenge them.

These two campaigns of Sam's began as experiments in self-development. On both fronts there was the need to show women as trustworthy without asking for proof, and also to demonstrate, once and for all, the inherent dignity of women as made in the image of God.

The third tradition Sam attacked was the practice of early marriage for young girls. A girl would often be married off between the ages of 11 and 14 to a 20- or even 50-year-old man, leading to painful sexual consequences and early pregnancies. It also meant the added responsibility of a family and children which a young woman at that age had little ability to cope with. These marriages were all arranged; freedom of choice was non-existent. Sam decided to fight the practice.

Once again, he wrote an article in his magazine condemning the custom, arguing that women should be consulted over who they were to marry, and when. They should not be blindly told what to do and accept the word of men in who their choice of husband should be. Reaction was swift.

A local 13-year-old girl was being forced to marry her uncle, her father's brother, now in his late forties, following the death of his wife. The man had gone to the girl's home and spoken with her parents, and they had agreed on the marriage. They would not force a confrontation and face splitting the family by refusing the uncle. Arrangements were made for the wedding and the transaction was concluded between the parents and the uncle.

Dismayed, the girl, now newly literate through the village literacy programme, had no wish to be married to her uncle. She read the article Sam had written in *Risalet El-Noor* and showed it to the pastor of her church, and pleaded for his help. The girl had other plans for her future, and they did not include being married to this uncle.

The pastor admired the girl's daring and her willingness to talk about the problem publicly, and he said he would help. The girl then ran to her mother and showed her the article, saying that it had been written by a qasis (pastor) and therefore she had a right to be asked about who she should marry. After considerable argument her mother agreed, but said she still had to convince her father.

Emboldened by all the support she was getting, the girl approached her father and his brother the man who wanted to marry her and made her feelings known. A fearful verbal battle followed. The girl ran and brought in the pastor to intervene. By now the whole village knew about the arranged marriage and the fight the girl was carrying on.

From Sam's perspective this couldn't have been better. New habits and new ideas are best spread by word of mouth, and the village grapevine worked well in this instance. The girl's stance against marrying her uncle had spread like wildfire throughout the village, as nothing is ever really kept secret or private in village life. Soon everybody knew about it. The issue was being confronted by a single girl, and if she was prepared to make a stand, and hopefully win, then other girls would follow her example. A precedent was being set that would break centuries-old traditions and establish a trend for the future. Sam prayed that people's attitudes would change, and himself did all he could to make this happen.

When the furore finally died down, a ruling was made. The wedding was cancelled. This was not only a personal triumph for Sam; it was a strike against centuries-old customs and a victory for the girls of the whole village, as well as for future generations of women. It was a quantum leap in the right direction, and soon the word spread to other nearby communities about the girl's victory. With Sam's help, she had struck an unprecedented blow for women's dignity and freedom. Liberated by the verdict she had fought so hard for, the girl later went on to marry a man she really loved and became a leader in the community, teaching others to read and write.

Sam's approach to these Herculean problems was judged a success even by his critics, and in time others would follow his lead. Today, in most of the big cities of Egypt the practices of female circumcision and proving a girl's virginity have all but vanished, and only arranged marriages continue. In the villages and among poor urban communities these practices still continue, but they are slowly dying.

Sam's sermon topics continued to hammer away at themes he felt were relevant to everyday village life. He preached on the role of women in the home, in the family, in the church and in society. He taught women how to care for their children and to deepen their relationships with their menfolk. He was convinced of the need for salvation of the whole person: body, mind and spirit. No aspect of life was left untouched. It was a revolution the like of which had never been seen before: it was total conversion.

Soon Sam's ideas and the changes he sought spread to other

villages, like Manhari in the same province. Sam Habib was urging people to go against thoroughly ingrained patterns of thinking and living, and in doing so repudiate their own cultural history. Inviting men and women steeped in convention and superstition to face and deal with centuries-old traditions was not easy, and Sam faced continual scorn and deep opposition for the stands he was taking. But Sam, undaunted, was insistent: there would be no going back, no return to the past.

In 1958 Sam sought out another deprived village on the east bank of the River Nile, Deir al-Barsha, with more than 12,000 inhabitants. Sam's hope was to make it the second largest literacy experiment in Egypt. He launched out into a full-scale literacy programme. Almost immediately it blossomed.

Literacy classes were held for women in the morning and men in the evening after they had completed their day's work. Over 1,000 adults enrolled in the programme, and the results exceeded everybody's expectations. The literacy programme created hundreds of new readers and a new level of literacy was attained among the villagers, marking a milestone in village education.

Deir al-Barsha was a totally Christian community. There were three Christian denominations present: Coptic Orthodox, the Evangelical Church and the Plymouth Brethren. All joined actively in the campaign to bring about literacy. In the evenings, church services were held out on the desert with upwards of 2,000 coming to hear the gospel preached and to worship.

Women came bearing lamps to show the way in the dark streets, as the village had no public electricity at that time. At the meetings presentations were also made about how to improve village conditions and life in general. Sam's intent was to show the holistic nature of the gospel to men and women as they had never heard it before. He challenged their centuries-old community traditions in the name of the One who came to bring freedom and redemption.

One notable change was in raising the prestige and role of women in the home and in the church. More and more, women were listened to by their menfolk and no longer ignored. Clearly, if women could read and write and own and operate small businesses, they deserved to be listened to. Girls, too, were now beginning to be consulted about the men they would marry and given the freedom to accept or reject the men being chosen for them.

The centuries-old practice of female circumcision was discussed openly for the first time, and declared irrational, wrong, unhygienic and harmful to the long-term health of women. But the decision to abandon such practices always came about as a result of community discussions. Nothing was ever imposed on the village from the outside.

In another completely radical move, Sam called upon the churches in the village to tear down the partition wall that separated men and women, so that both sexes could openly worship God together. Sam challenged the idea that if men and women worshipped alongside each other men might be tempted with lustful thoughts. If men could work alongside women in the fields ten hours a day, then why couldn't they worship alongside each other in the church for two hours on Sunday? Sam's argument eventually prevailed, and many, though not all, of the churches tore down their partitions. Nevertheless, it was a step in the right direction as far as Sam was concerned.

In other communities, where there was a higher proportion of Muslims to Christians, the issues were different and the problems were therefore addressed differently. As the programme expanded and changed, Sam saw the need to change the name of the organization. At his suggestion the committee modified its name and called itself Literacy and Christian Literature, concentrating solely on Egypt and from now on excluding Sudan.

The latest literacy experiment had proved a tremendous success, and in 1958 Sam initiated a Bible study campaign in Deiral-Barsha for those made newly literate through the programme. His purpose was to make every literate Christian person a Bible reader. Then, and only then, would they be able to understand the Word of God for themselves and discern His will for their lives.

The first books were prepared, and the first Bible study campaign ever to take place in the village began, with the backing of all three churches. It proved enormously successful. The Bible used was an Arabic translation made by Van Dyke, a Presbyterian missionary to Lebanon in the 18th century, and brought to Egypt by Presbyterian missionaries in 1854. On this occasion, it was sold to the people for 20 piastres (about five cents U.S.), fifty percent of what it cost to produce. The committee lost money, but reaped a harvest of souls. More than 1,000 adult men and women took part in this bold experiment and in time became Bible readers.

Dr. Floyd Shacklock, who was at that time General Secretary of the NCCC Committee on World Literacy and Christian Literature, flew in from the United States to view the experiment and was pleased with what he saw. As a result he increased the contributions coming from 'Lit-Lit' into the programme to cover the needs of the new campaign.

Shacklock would be remembered with affection in the community for another reason, too. The agricultural centre at the Presbyterian mission-run Assiut College nearby used to import Jersey cattle from the United States for cross-breeding to improve local stock. While Floyd Shacklock was visiting Sam's literacy and Bible study programmes, a Jersey bull arrived in the village from Assiut. It was at once named 'Shacklock', to the great delight of the whole community.

What started out in 1952 as a bold experiment in literacy, with little hope of acceptance or success, now proved in 1958 to be a highly successful method by which the churches could begin to teach the Bible. The key was literacy, and Sam had proven it could be successfully done even among Egypt's poorest.

By now leaders of the broader church community in Egypt were beginning to see the importance of what Sam was doing and the general impact it was having on the church and for the people. But it would not be till the late 1960s that church leaders from all the denominations would see its vital importance for the church's overall task and ministry and act on what they saw by fully endorsing and supporting it. It was one thing to see the extent of the programme's success, and the promise it held for countless Egyptians; it was another matter entirely for the church to embrace the whole task of tackling illiteracy and make it a part of its own programme.

From his reading of Scripture, especially the four gospels, Sam's understanding of his own role and mission became clearer. In the story of the ten lepers recorded in Luke's gospel, Sam saw a paradigm of his own calling. Jesus healed ten men with leprosy, but only one returned to thank him. There is no record that Jesus even presented the gospel to the others. He cured them because he saw their value as human beings. That was important enough to Jesus. He needed no other reason than simply their need to be healed, regardless of whether they saw him as their Messiah and Saviour. The one who came back and thanked him was given another chance to know who Jesus was and to believe in him.

Later, with his successes firmly established, Sam began to explore new relationships with Muslims too, as he began working in their communities. He needed a model for doing this. He had already faced criticism from his denomination merely about assisting Orthodox Christians, and now he planned to work among Muslims. This, he knew, would bring down a torrent of criticism on his head that would be even harder to bear. But Sam was determined. He would struggle for what was right, whatever the personal cost.

In Jesus, he saw one who reached out to all those around him regardless of race, colour or religion. Jesus was race- and colour-blind, seeing men and women in their physical and spiritual need and rescuing them. Jesus reserved his harshest condemnation for the religious leaders of his day. They were the real hypocrites. Jesus was at ease with a Samaritan woman, a Roman soldier, a Jewish tax collector, a prostitute, an adulterer and a self-righteous Rabbi. Not all who saw and listened to him confessed faith in him as the promised Messiah; yet Jesus reached out to all with love and compassion, seeing them in their need and healing them.

This would be Sam's model. He would not confine his ministry to Christians only. Muslims had the same right to love, justice and mercy as Christians did. Jesus was no respecter of persons, so neither would Sam be. It was a bold stand, and one not entirely welcomed or understood by the Christian churches. But Sam stood firm.

Already, by the late 1950s, Sam began to see that literacy programmes were not enough. More, much more, needed to be done for Egypt's poor. He saw the need for other forms of education and assistance for the poor people he worked with to develop their lives more fully.

He made a chart which spelled out the need not only for continuing literacy and Bible study programmes but also for broader educational and service programmes that included preventive healthcare and agricultural and economic development.

When he first presented his chart to local church leaders he was met with scorn and derision. One by one they said it couldn't be done. 'Impossible,' they said. It would need a 'millionaire uncle' to pull it off. At that time annual contributions to the literacy project totalled $12,000, most of it coming from Lit-Lit, the World Literacy Commission of the NCCC. $12,000 was a princely sum in those days, but Sam realized he would need an additional $30,000 a year for all of his new projects to get off the ground. He prayed and then stepped out in a bold act of faith, trusting that God would lead and guide his efforts.

He presented the proposal to the Presbyterian Church Women (U.S.A.) and they promptly accepted it. Perhaps it was his fearless efforts on behalf of Egypt's women that prompted their approval. Whatever it was, the request was made through the American Mission in Egypt, quickly found its way to the United States and was promptly endorsed. Sam had taken a leap of faith. He had seen the need and heeded the call, and God had answered. Later, 'Lit-Lit' passed the entire bill over to the Presbyterian Church (U.S.A.) and the denomination picked up the cost in full for the whole programme.

With these new programmes in place, Sam was joined in Minia by the Rev. Dr. John G. (Jack) Lorimer, an American Presbyterian missionary based in Cairo. He was invited to share the leadership with Sam and a number of other missionaries and the renowned New Testament scholar Rev. Dr. Kenneth E. Bailey. The full-time staff of the programme was increased from twenty to forty.

Sam began the first multi-pronged experiment to help Egypt's indigent with a flourish of development activities. He immediately contacted the United Nations Educational, Scientific and Cultural Organization (UNESCO) leaders at Sirs al-Layaan in the Nile Delta, in Lower Egypt. They had completed an abundance of theoretical and scientific study on the problems but lacked the practical dimension.

Sam and his colleagues had learned their method of operation by watching UNESCO's experiments. Their programme was now beginning to shape up as a full community development programme. UNESCO leaders visited Sam to see the basis of his success. What they saw amazed them. Sam's team of workers was not only benefiting from their scientific research, but also winning a positive public response.

Nevertheless, the team was now beginning from scratch with a new development programme. Almost immediately this attracted the government's attention. Their growth and success had finally blossomed sufficiently for them to be noticed by more than just the churches. Sam realized that the programme would probably now have to make it on its own, independent of the Evangelical Church.

Up until now they had remained a committee of the Evangelical (Presbyterian) Church, but by 1960 they had become big enough to be recognized by the Egyptian government, and as such had to be registered under the Ministry of Social Affairs.

But life was not standing still for Sam in other, more personal, areas of his life. In 1955, at the age of 27, he had married a young woman from Cairo, Fawzia Fahim Ayad. They had met a few years earlier, fallen in love and become engaged in 1954, one month before Sam had gone to the United States. Once he returned to Egypt, Sam was anxious to be married.

Fawzia was a teacher at Ramses College for Girls, formerly a Presbyterian College and now under the Synod of the Nile. She had grown up in a Christian family among godly Presbyterians. Both her parents were converts from the Coptic Orthodox Church.

Fawzia had taken a course in biblical studies while at the same time serving in various communities near where she lived in Cairo, and had been active in her church from an early age. She had studied at the Emmanuel Centre in Cairo, an institution reserved for the development of women's leadership in the church, and had become the centre's librarian. The couple met at a meeting Sam had called for church librarians in Cairo. Sam noticed her immediately and they began to date.

On December 15, 1955, they were married in the Ezbekiya Church, Cairo, by the pastor Dr. Gabriel Rizkallah who from the time Sam had entered seminary had been like a father to him. More than 700 attended the wedding, which was a very dignified affair compared with the often rowdy weddings more typical of Egyptian society. Both Sam and Fawzia were 27, and together they felt the call of God on their lives. Fawzia's life would now be bound up with Sam's life and ministry. They would act as one.

Their union was in harmony with all that Sam believed and knew God wanted for his life, and Fawzia saw herself fitting into the Divine Plan for both of them. She would share her husband's vision and play an active role in the ministry that lay ahead for him. She would teach and initiate Bible studies wherever they went and participate in women's activities within the church.

The hectic life that Sam and Fawzia would share together for the rest of their lives became apparent even on their honeymoon. On the fourth day of their new life together, Sam received a call at the hotel where they were staying from an American film crew that had flown in from the United States. They were anxious to make a film about his work, and had a week to shoot the film and be on their way.

Not to offend the 'intruders', Sam and his new bride set off with the film crew back to the village of Deir Abu Hinnis. For a week they endured dusty floors, tainted well water and the risk of endemic village diseases while the film company shot its footage.

The week in the village was an education for Fawzia, who had never before visited Upper Egypt, seen a village or observed her husband's work. It gave her new insights into the future she would share with this energetic, driven and yet humble man, as for the first time she saw the extent of his educational and development programmes. From now on, Fawzia would be Sam's right-hand person, critiquing and evaluating his performance and keeping him focused on the needs of others as she saw his vision unfold.

The next few years were hectic ones for the young bride. In addition to learning her new role as wife of the dynamic Samuel Habib, she now became a homemaker. She also became very active in the church at both the local and national level. Her skills marked her out as a leader, and later she headed the Women's Union of the Evangelical Church in Egypt for nine years. Over time she established two nurseries in Cairo and helped churches outside of Cairo establish their own nurseries, where women could leave their children to be educated while the mothers went out to work.

From their marriage Sam and Fawzia have two children. A daughter, Rosana, was born in 1957, and two years later a son, Rafik. Rosana studied pharmacy, later marrying a pharmacist. Rafik received his Ph.D. in social psychology at the age of 27, and is today a researcher on development and an evaluator of CEOSS programmes. Both children reflect their parents' keen, analytical minds and concern for their father's ministry.

Sam's marriage marked another milestone in the history of his life, and a profound one. Sam Habib had taken another giant step forward, and had seen the faithfulness of God working in all his endeavours.

A vision of what he could do was stirring in his mind and he was anxious to move on.

Chapter 4

CEOSS is Born

By September 1960, Sam's fledgling work in literacy and Bible study programmes had begun to carry over into other areas of much-needed development in the villages. Land reclamation, home economics, education, agriculture and health care now became additional targets of his concern.

As the programme's growth became apparent to the Evangelical churches across Egypt, it was decided by a vote of the Synod of the Nile that Sam should no longer be under the Synod's authority but launch out on his own with a new and separate ministry altogether. They would support him, but they made it clear that he now stood alone.

His new-found visibility also caught the attention of the government, and so Sam applied to the Ministry of Social Affairs to register under the name of the Coptic Evangelical Organization for Social Services (CEOSS), an independent, non-profit social service organization designed to serve all communities, Christian and Muslim alike. The government quickly recognized the new organization.

When someone once asked him how he came up with CEOSS's lengthy title, Sam replied that he simply put Arabic and English names together to make one English acronym, and CEOSS was it. He also chose the name to denote CEOSS's relationship with the Evangelical Church from which it had come, which he had every intention of preserving, and the goal of social services to which he and the new organization were now committed.

It was the dawn of a new day for himself and CEOSS. He moved quickly to put the organization firmly on the map. He was joined in his new venture by a number of American missionaries and Egyptian nationals, men and women who had seen the vision Sam Habib was describing and wanted to be part of it. Once the identity of CEOSS was in place, he brought together a number of established Christian leaders to form its first board, in order to make CEOSS both responsible and accountable to its constituency and, of course, to the ever-present government bureaucracy.

As an agency registered with the government, CEOSS could now claim both tax and customs exemptions. It also meant that monies coming from abroad had to be approved by the ministry and used for the purposes stated. It also meant annual auditing, and to that end Sam hired one of the best auditors in the country in the person of Dr. Hanna Youssef Hanna, a prominent auditor who worked with national and international organizations in Egypt, to audit CEOSS's books.

It was a good move and a perfect match of organization and auditor. Over the next thirty-three years the Ministry of Social Affairs never once questioned or objected to the way CEOSS received or spent its monies. But the temptation to accept money from any source had to be vigorously resisted.

At one time an American fundamentalist organization supporting the Zionist Movement in Israel and with strong ties to that state wanted to give CEOSS $20,000 a year in perpetuity. In offering Sam and CEOSS the money it sought, in return, an endorsement of its principles and policies regarding the Middle East and what they viewed as God's prophetic plan for the Jews, excluding of course, Christian and Muslim Arabs. Sam refused point blank. Tempting as it was to accept such a large sum of money, which CEOSS desperately needed, he was not prepared to compromise his principles or those of CEOSS for anyone with money in their hands, least of all a group of American fundamentalists who blindly believed Israel had the Biblical and God-sanctioned right to pursue some millennial plan, even if it meant seizing Arab lands and killing Arabs, many of whom were Christians, in the process. Sam would do nothing to compromise CEOSS's charter or to violate its standing with the Egyptian people, especially Christians; nor would he adapt his theology to suit a group of American dispensationalists just for money. He would not risk the good relationships he had established with Egypt's churches, especially the Synod of the Nile, or the cooperation he had sought and won with the government. Too much was at stake.

From the very beginning it was an uphill battle for CEOSS as Sam sought recognition from churches and denominations, most of whom did not care to support his social ministry ideas. To get those churches involved in literacy work had been difficult enough; to get them now involved in a broader plan for social outreach was a much harder call.

One Christian leader, however, who stood by Sam in his struggles through the early years was his old mentor, friend and confidant Dr. Labib Mishriqi, who saw Sam's vision, understood and supported it. On the day CEOSS was registered, Mishriqi became its first board chairman and continued in that role for many years. (He died on January 16, 1990.) Whenever doubts assailed him, Sam would turn to Mishriqi for wisdom and guidance. The older man shared the younger man's vision for Egypt's poor, realizing that God had, in a very special way, placed his hand on Sam's life.

There was work now to be done and, regardless of what people thought or said, Sam knew what he had to do. Because of his training and his orderly cast of mind, Sam immediately set about organizing CEOSS into sectors (see chart on page xx), each with its own distinctive objectives. He initially set up two.

The first sector was the publishing house Dar El Thaqafa, which printed materials for two audiences. The first set of materials was for CEOSS's development programmes, such as books for the new reading public on community health, agriculture, economics, women's concerns, family life and child-rearing.

The second set of materials were Christian books; magazines, theological textbooks and other reference materials for the wider Christian community in order to nurture the church. Sam was determined that a major focus of the publishing house should be to help people understand the Word of God and apply it intelligently to the issues of the world they lived in.

The publishing house grew rapidly, and by 1993 it had nine bookshops across the country, six of them in Cairo and one each in the cities of Minia, Alexandria and Assiut. In addition, CEOSS contracted with many other outlets throughout Egypt to distribute its Christian literature.

In the mid-1980s the publishing house embarked on a major publishing venture, that of preparing and printing a six-volume Encyclopedia of Biblical Knowledge. To date four volumes have been printed, and the mammoth task of completing and publishing all six volumes is expected to be achieved by the year 2000. The publishing house is also engaged in printing many other original writings and translating quality English books into Arabic. Between sixty and seventy new titles, including both first editions and reprints, roll off the printing presses each year.

The second sector involved development. Under Sam's guidance CEOSS immediately set about initiating new programmes in literacy, home economics, and agricultural activities such as the cross-breeding of cattle and providing farmers with newly-bred chickens.

CEOSS at first focused its efforts in the urban and rural communities of Minia and Assiut provinces, later extending the work to four other provinces including the capital, Cairo. Until now CEOSS had gone for mainly Christian communities, of which there are very few in Egypt as most communities are mixed, usually with a Muslim majority. In 1960, however, Sam began work in the predominantly Muslim community of Ben-Adi, the first Muslim community CEOSS set foot in.

From now on CEOSS would work in such communities as well, always with an eye to establishing better relations between Muslims and Christians and insisting on serving the total community, showing no partiality to either group's desire to achieve a better life. This was a pattern he would repeat over and over again.

The model of the Good Samaritan remained firmly fixed in his mind, as did Jesus's encounter with the woman at the well. Jesus showed no partiality as to whom he chose to heal and save. Neither would Sam.

Sam insisted that his call was to serve the poor whoever and wherever they were, without religious distinction. He argued that a community was one single unit regardless of who it was made up of, and CEOSS would serve the whole community regardless of the religious make-up of the people in it. He would never divide the community into two entities and serve only one.

It took Sam some time, of course, to win acceptance for what CEOSS was doing. Education was needed on all sides: not only for Muslim villagers to accept Christian help, but also for local churches to accept that eighty percent or more of the beneficiaries of some of CEOSS's programmes were Muslims.

The Evangelical Church had found it hard enough in the early days to support work with non-Evangelical Christians, such as predominantly Coptic Orthodox communities. But Sam was aware that a number of inter-denominational marriages had taken place, so that even within families some members might be Orthodox and others Evangelical. Serving the total community, therefore, was not merely an option but an absolute necessity. Now the work was opening up to people of all religious affiliations, and everyone had to get used to it.

CEOSS was now clearly identified as an independent organization, registered and recognized by the state and accountable to its own independent board. This gave it the freedom to formulate its own policies and develop its own programme, and to receive monies and spend them without outside control or interference. Nevertheless, Sam desperately wanted CEOSS to maintain active and friendly relations with the Evangelical Church of Egypt.

CEOSS now began to experiment with courses in home economics for women and girls, unprecedented in Egyptian family life. Women in Egypt's rural villages needed training and support in such fundamental areas as home management and economics, nutrition, disease prevention, sewing and other valuable skills.

By focusing on home economics CEOSS was able to open a whole new dimension in the training of women in the home. This also benefited husbands, who often saw their wives as little more than chattels, and children, who often suffered at the hands of parental neglect and ignorance, especially in areas of health care and nutrition.

An estimated forty percent of rural Egyptian households live below the poverty line, weaving economic disadvantage in a net that traps families who lack the resources to better themselves. Women are the vital and often only link and asset in the economy of the home. Helping girls and women aged 12 to 60 just to become better economizers was and remains an essential key to raising the living standards of their households, sometimes making the difference between empty stomachs and having enough.

None of this was easy. It was grass roots work all the way. Home economics classes would be geared not only for women and girls, but also seek the involvement of their menfolk. Sometimes husbands and fathers would attend sessions to enable them to see what their wives and daughters were studying and provide encouragement at home.

CEOSS also pioneered new programmes of educational and cultural activities for women, children and youth to help them build stronger personal foundations for their future. The more education they got, the more informed the decisions they could make about their choice of work and how and where they lived, and the easier they would find it to take steps towards a better life in society. Literacy and learning were the keys to their future.

This was 'the decade of development', and through CEOSS Sam sought to expand the role of women in society. To this end CEOSS initiated a massive education programme to expand the role of women both in the church and in communities. CEOSS not only empowered women to serve in their own communities but also enabled them to sit on councils and to be involved in decision-making at all levels of their personal lives, in their families, the church and society. Women were taught in classroom discussions and through public meetings and preaching that they could and should take their rightful place alongside men and be treated as equals.

Sam Habib was breaking entirely new ground, and he knew that by doing so he would be violating age-old practices. The resistance he encountered, much of it from the churches, seemed at times overwhelming. But Sam was determined to carry on regardless.

In the early 1960s CEOSS, now firmly established, began a massive programme of health care, the first of its kind ever to be carried out on such a scale in Egyptian villages. The first thing CEOSS did was to launch massive clean-up campaigns involving cleaning sewers, streets and homes, and building latrines in homes where none existed.

CEOSS also initiated the first-ever comprehensive programmes of both preventive health measures and clinical/ medical treatment to stave off endemic diseases and provide long-term health care. CEOSS brought in doctors to all the communities to treat endemic diseases, and where that was not possible CEOSS took sick people out of the communities and sent them to doctors' clinics in other areas. The programme reached not only into rural communities but into urban areas as well. CEOSS was now beginning to move into high gear.

Sam then established a third CEOSS sector, one of agricultural projects to help farmers develop better methods of farming. In 1974 CEOSS organized a dairy farm (Prince Farm) in the rural district of Prinsat, 30 miles north of Minia; and a few miles to the south, closer to Minia, a nursery for tree farming was set up at a place called Itsa.

As well as purchasing better strains of cattle and better quality chickens, CEOSS added a beehive project to help farmers take up beekeeping, or honey farming. Each participating farmer was given seven beehives, on the understanding that he would be able to double them in a year. The process was then repeated with new farmers each year, providing them with a new source of income from the sale of honey. The earnings generated by just seven hives equalled the income a local farmer could make from working one acre of land.

Within a short space of time Sam added a fourth sector, running centres set up for the purpose of training CEOSS staff and other leaders, Christian and Muslim, in various spheres of work such as health care, family planning, agriculture, literacy and special pro-grammes for the training of clergy in theological studies, pastoral practices and development concepts. Because of Sam's background in journalism he also set about providing special training for writers.

In addition to a permanently moored houseboat on the Nile at Minia which served as its first training and hospitality centre, CEOSS built a centre ten miles away at Itsa which could accom-modate 150 men and women for training purposes. Because of the extraordinary demand for leadership training in Egypt, a third centre is presently planned for construction in Maadi, a suburb of Cairo, which when completed will accommodate more than 300 people fully utilized.

As CEOSS grew and its ministry expanded, Sam saw the need to bring together vocational training with a real profit-making business venture. CEOSS thus launched a fifth sector in 1980, with the title of General Services, which opened a carpentry business called Itsa Wood, based at the Itsa Centre, producing high-quality made-to-order furniture. CEOSS opened two showrooms, in Minia and Suhag in Upper Egypt, where customers can walk in off the street, select the furniture they want from catalogues, choose the fabric and wood, pay and leave. The order is promptly sent to Itsa Wood and a team of carpenters, some of them trainees and others with long experience, immediately begin constructing and assembling the furniture. Within a matter of weeks the furniture is completed and personally delivered to the buyer.

In the early 1980s Sam also formed CEO-Press by purchasing a high-quality printing facility with computerized typesetting to print some of the literature needed for various CEOSS programmes. By 1995 the organization was housed in new premises and a large high-speed printing press installed. In addition to meeting CEOSS's own needs it also has the ability to print materials for other agencies. CEOSS is also developing capabilities for producing audio-visual materials, including photo printing and video production, to keep pace with the fast-changing world of electronic communications.

In 1981 CEOSS established a sixth sector, for the purpose of rehabilitating some of Egypt's vast number of disabled people. An estimated four percent of Egypt's nearly 59 million people are disabled from birth, sometimes as a result of genetic defects from marriages within the same family. Because of long-standing prejudices and social indifference, the disabled are often seen as a source of embarrassment and shame to their families. CEOSS is sensitive to all these problems and is endeavouring, through programmes of education, to change people's attitudes to disability and the disabled.

Two 'Better Life' Centres, one in Cairo and the other in Minia, were opened to train men and women to work among the disabled. Initially the centres were set up to focus on rehabilitating the disabled themselves, but later the emphasis shifted towards training people to work in communities and serve disabled people where they live. CEOSS also launched a vocational training programme for the disabled to equip them for finding jobs. Empowering people, especially the disabled, to support themselves became a central theme for all of CEOSS's ministries.

Beginning in the 1970s, CEOSS saw a new and emerging problem in Egypt: a population exploding out of control and still increasing today at the rate of one million new mouths to feed every nine months. By the year 2000, it is estimated, the population will be over 66 million.

President Nasser had already begun talking about family planning during his years as president, but it was President Sadat and his wife Jehan in the 1970s who threw their combined weight behind the movement, putting the issue firmly on the map with their support. When President Mubarak took office in 1981 he pressed the case even more strongly for parents to have smaller families.

CEOSS first initiated a programme of birth control to help

mothers who already had several children to limit the number of new babies, starting with a campaign of education. Then in 1974 it began a full programme to meet all the family planning needs of people in the villages.

Sam knew that in launching these new programmes CEOSS was going against centuries-old superstitions and traditions. For these programmes to work, CEOSS had to link them to a full programme of overall development. Birth control had to be taught in conjunction with broader programmes of education and service to the community. To separate out birth control from the total context of health care would have meant certain rejection by village leaders. Furthermore, it was essential that overall health care be improved for both women and children if the programme was to succeed. By the 1990's CEOSS moved into Community Based Rehabilitation (CBR). This meant that CEOSS's services did not depend on centres. They were now being carried out in communities where the disabled live with their families and CEOSS could now help the communities deal with them.

To acquire the expertise he needed Sam, in 1974, sought out information from the National Population Council, NPC (formerly called the Family Planning Council) and the International Planned Parenthood Federation (IPPF). He began studying family planning in earnest, and summarized his thinking in a book he wrote on the subject, *A Christian View of Family Planning.*

He then invited Bishop Samuel of the Coptic Orthodox Church to write an article on the subject which CEOSS published and distributed to Orthodox families. Sam also invited Muslim leaders to write about the subject from an Islamic point of view. Not content with religious leaders pontificating on the subject, he then arranged for a number of public forums and open meetings with panels of speakers including Muslim imams, Coptic Orthodox priests, Catholic priests and Evangelical pastors to discuss the whole subject.

Delicate as the subject was, and embarrassing as it might be to discuss such a topic in public, thousands of people nevertheless showed up to hear what the religious leaders had to say. None of the leaders issued ultimatums; nor was anyone coerced into family planning, as had been the case in India for a brief period and later in China. Any decisions made by people in Egypt were personal and private. But these public meetings got people thinking. The net result was that CEOSS became one of the most successful organizations in Egypt in implementing effective family planning.

Sam observed that there was a real correlation between increased wealth and smaller families. As economic conditions for families improved, the number of children they had automatically declined. For Sam it was clear that CEOSS had to package family planning with overall economic development in village communities. A multi-level approach was the only way a community could grow and develop.

By the late 1970s CEOSS had put into place a system of loans and grants to assist Egypt's poor, along with vocational training and education. Major programmes were implemented to help poor individuals select some kind of craft that would enable them to carve out a living for themselves. At the same time interest-free loans of a few hundred dollars were made to individuals, and up to three or four thousand dollars to groups, after a scientific feasibility study had been done to see if the project had a chance of succeeding.

Co-operatives were established to build much-needed bakeries and carpentry shops. CEOSS provided loans for poor people to buy shares in the co-operative. Once the projects became profitable CEOSS was reimbursed from a percentage of the income, and the monies were turned over to new people and projects. Loans for community-owned projects often reached $7,000, and occasionally went as high as $50,000.

The loan programme was a huge success. Initial loans and seed money not only allowed people to develop small businesses, but also gave them enough to support themselves while they started up. Over time, as businesses prospered, the money was repaid and new loans were made to other needy families to assist them in making new starts for themselves. Tens of thousands of men and women, both Muslim and Christian, were given the opportunity to become entrepreneurs and develop their lives in new and creative ways.

As CEOSS approached the 1980s the complexities of the growing organization, and the need to ensure that new programmes got off the ground successfully, demanded more and better trained staff. What Sam needed for the new structure of CEOSS was college-educated men and women who were experienced and trained in such areas as health care, management, leadership training, publishing and editing, theology and comparative religion, vocational training, micro-economic development, income generation, literacy and, later, community organization.

In its recruitment, therefore, CEOSS from now on looked to university graduates, rather than those coming out of high school, for its next generation of leaders. Better qualified and trained personnel in CEOSS meant that in time they would be able to make responsible on-the-spot decisions in the field, thus allowing the organization to decentralize management decisions.

Applications were invited and resumes poured in from people from all walks of life. CEOSS was now well established and had committees in place to screen applications and make the choices it needed. CEOSS did not want to rely solely on length of experience to build up a new generation of decision-makers. Nor did it discriminate by age or gender in its employment and promotion of personnel at any level, aiming rather for a balance of men and women of various ages.

The organization therefore concentrated on finding the kind of personnel it needed and their ability to pick up on an idea, run with it, fulfil its objectives and then move on to the next project. The key quality Sam demanded when hiring any person was professionalism. Was the person qualified for the job that had to be done? If the answer was yes, they were hired.

Although CEOSS was now looking for graduates, the subject they graduated in was not important. They could be trained. The educational background of the current senior management team ranges from engineering and theology to arts, health, psychology, agriculture, English literature, management and commerce. What was important was that they had a graduate-level education and knew how to think through the issues. Sam began training these men and women for top level management in CEOSS.

To obtain the kind of trained men and women Sam wanted, however, also meant sending a number of CEOSS staff to further their studies both locally and abroad to acquire more training and become better qualified. Some went to the UNESCO centre in the Nile Delta to take courses. Sam also sent several staff abroad for further education in economics, management, accountancy, agriculture, development and theology. Several went to Canada, England and the United States to obtain further diplomas and degrees. The Presbyterian Church (U.S.A.) assisted CEOSS, as did the World Council of Churches, in providing scholarships. Other international agencies from Europe also assisted CEOSS in setting up a scholarship fund for staff to study and train abroad.

When CEOSS began its work in Egypt in the 1950s and 60s, it took the lead in moving away from a traditional social work approach towards a more developmental method.

Traditional social work in Egypt was basically institutional. This meant the construction of buildings where people lived; orphanages, for example, together with all the necessary support personnel and staff. This approach, which tended to isolate those served from their communities, had been the traditional style of social work in Egypt; in fact it was an approach fairly common throughout most industrialized nations of the world, regardless of whether the government or private social agencies did most of the social work.

What CEOSS did, however, beginning in the 1950s, was to move away from this traditional, segregationist approach into being a social service agency providing communities with the services they needed. A poor community would seek the services of CEOSS and CEOSS would respond by moving in to help it. CEOSS took an integrated, community-based approach, working with people where they were, serving them where they lived, and for the most part circumventing the need for institutions or new buildings.

For example, home cleanliness and hygiene were important factors in helping people obtain a better quality of life, and CEOSS's programmes always began with this before moving on to more general areas of education. Programmes were nearly always conducted in the home, in a familiar environment, which proved much more effective than the traditional, formal approach.

If there was a need for classes CEOSS chose rooms in homes, or used as classrooms buildings that were already available without paying money to build new ones. If some of the buildings needed renovation, a new window pane or two perhaps, CEOSS would see to it. This was something new for Egypt: a non-traditional, informal system where literacy programmes could take place in a non-threatening atmosphere, a far cry from the official system of classrooms, buildings and students with a regular curriculum.

CEOSS never moved far from the life of the people. So when it came to a village it didn't set up buildings and institutions; it brought ideas and activities. If someone asked where CEOSS was, Sam replied that CEOSS was a movement, an idea, not a building with a sign advertising itself. This approach saved vast sums of money that would otherwise have been spent on administration and management, and instead put money directly into programmes and ultimately into the hands of the people. They were the ultimate beneficiaries. One could also work in more communities and reach out to more people through CEOSS's methods than through traditional institutions. An institution could cater for only a small number of people, and an enormous amount of money was needed to maintain it.

Yet while the community approach is certainly much cheaper to implement than the institutional model, it is not necessarily easier. It was, as Sam frequently found, much more difficult. It needs to build community support, for one thing. Whenever CEOSS begins work in a new area, it sets about making sure that all groups and agencies in the community are involved. They all participate in the programme and learn for themselves how it is to be done. Word quickly spreads around the community and people begin to come and see for themselves and to share in the programme.

CEOSS willingly taught other organizations how this new approach could be implemented, and in time, much to Sam's pleasure, other agencies began to copy CEOSS's methods, leading to thousands of people being lifted out of poverty.

These agencies included not only religious groups, like Orthodox and Catholic churches and Muslim organizations, but also government agencies and secular societies, associations and other private organizations. Some of them succeeded and some did not. Sadly, competition occasionally erupted within the community among some of the agencies, and this often proved damaging to the community. But on the whole it was a success.

One of CEOSS's fundamental approaches was to encourage volunteer leaders to do work without payment, for the good of the whole community. Unfortunately, other organizations would come in later and offer money to the leaders to attract them to their organizations. This undercut CEOSS's methods and approach, as CEOSS insisted on volunteer work and workers to rebuild the community. Also, some agencies would compete against one another with negative consequences. Sam always encouraged healthy competition if it helped people do better and enhance the community, but such was not always the case.

In the years that followed, CEOSS pioneered work among some of Egypt's poorest communities, the very poorest of the poor, places not reached by government services or any other agencies. They breathed new life into them with loan programmes, economic development and health and medical services.

Today CEOSS can point to more than five million people who have been directly helped by one CEOSS programme or another. For Sam, as he looks back, CEOSS is the triumph of a realized vision. But sitting back and resting on his laurels was not Sam Habib's style.

Times were changing. By the late 1970s the chronic problems of illiteracy, poverty and poor health in Egypt prompted Sam to re-evaluate CEOSS's whole programme. He saw the needs of Egypt's burgeoning poor growing at a rate faster than he could keep up with. But how was he to tackle the problem? A major reorganization of CEOSS was necessary.

In 1980 he invited an American living in Egypt to study CEOSS's entire programme, especially as it related to serving the poor. The results, after a three-month evaluation, revealed to Sam that he needed to point CEOSS in a completely new direction.

What emerged from the evaluation made Sam realize that CEOSS needed to adopt a development orientation rather than focus on providing social services. True to form, he quickly made the shift.

Within a few months CEOSS became the first and for a time only development-oriented organization in Egypt, a pioneer and model for other organizations to follow.

Today CEOSS is one of the rare organizations in the Third World that is completely and totally a development organization rather than a social service agency.

Acting quickly on the recommendations made by the American evaluator, Sam restructured what was then known as the Comprehensive Development programmes Sector of CEOSS, separating the functions of local community development (through what is now called the Local Development Division) and straightforward service provision (through what is now called the Specialized Services Division).

A special pre-studies office (later two, one in Cairo and one in Minia) was responsible for collecting information from the communities on those in need, evaluating the results and assisting those involved in the decision-making process. The question of whether CEOSS would or would not begin work in any new community depended totally on the results of the analysis done by these offices. On the information obtained from the community, CEOSS then decided whether or not it would move in and serve them.

One of the crucial resolutions Sam instituted for CEOSS was to follow a strict rule of never entering a community without first being invited. CEOSS received numerous invitations but only agreed to enter a community after careful study had been made showing a high degree of probability that its programme would succeed. Very little now was left to chance.

CEOSS would not deliberately reject a community if it did not meet all CEOSS's requirements. But at the same time it was felt that the community had to meet a number of minimum criteria necessary to make the kind of progress they and CEOSS envisaged. Once an invitation from a community had been accepted, CEOSS would set up a development committee and send resident staff to live in the community full-time and work closely with the people. Living in solidarity with the people was absolutely essential, Sam argued, if the programme was to work. This was all done in agreement with the community's leaders.

The committee was drawn up from officials of the community, and always included the mayor and head of the village council. It might also include a medical doctor or midwife, as well as Christian and Muslim religious leaders. The committee always included several women if possible, though this might take several months of education and persuasion. There would always be two CEOSS staff on the committee too. The CEOSS staff supervisor is known as the ra'is el balad (community chief). He is the key person, with the responsibility to ensure that the staff work properly together, to act as liaison with government officials and with the community committee, to sense what the morale of the community is at all times and to report on the issues as they emerge.

Members of the younger generation were also invited to sit on the committee, as many of the decisions made affected their lives and involved their futures. CEOSS and the committee would together then choose the programmes the community wanted, and go to work on the community's needs. It was made clear that the final decision about what should or should not be done in the community always rested with the committee. CEOSS would not impose itself.

Through its Department of Technical Services (forerunner of

the Specialized Services Division), CEOSS had a package of services it could provide. These included education and literacy programmes for adults and children, women's concerns, children's activities and Bible study for the churches and their members. In the area of health care, CEOSS offered community health programmes, preventive medicine, clinical services, insect eradication and community clean-up campaigns, as well as family planning and nutrition programmes. Loans and grants were made to individuals and groups, and an extensive agricultural programme including cattle cross-breeding and chicken-raising was offered to the community.

However, it was always up to the community to decide what it did and did not need. Priorities were always set by the community committee. An example of this occurred in a very poor community called El Hekr, in the heart of the city of Cairo, that lacked both clean water and a sewerage system. CEOSS was invited in to help the community obtain both. Over the years polluted water had brought disease and death to countless children, and the community leaders were becoming increasingly frustrated and angry with the lack of government action in doing anything about the situation. Because they were a very poor community they were low on the priority list of government concerns. They knew they would have to wait at least another ten to fifteen years before they would see clean water in their community. CEOSS agreed to pay fifty percent of the costs to put in a new water system. The government and the community each agreed to pay twenty-five percent.

Immediately CEOSS and the community went to work on the problems together. Within a matter of months the community had a clean water system and a sewage network. The success of the programme was a triumph for the people of the community, who had been involved in the whole process and seen their needs met. CEOSS had reached out to those in need, to the poorest of the poor, to those not reached by anyone else, and in Sam's mind not only was the community helped and lives saved but God was glorified by what was achieved.

One of the keys to the success of any project, Sam learned early on, was the need for full-time CEOSS workers to live and work in the community at least four days a week. In this way CEOSS became fully integrated into the community, with its staff on call day and night by the people in the community. Furthermore, by living in the community they became partners together with those they served. As an integrated unit they lived as one family doing the work together.

When Sam talks about development to both his colleagues and development experts he explains that it must come from within the local community using whatever resources it has, and he insists on actual participation by the community at all levels of decision-making. He always views CEOSS as an outside arm working in partnership with the community, assisting it to develop itself by looking at its own needs. CEOSS stays with a community anywhere from five to ten years then it withdraws to let local leaders and the community develop on their own.

From the 1980s onward CEOSS engaged extensively in community organization and comprehensive development programmes in approximately twenty 'partnership communities' at any one time, always under the watchful eye of the communities' leaders, working with the local committee to identify problems and prioritize needs, while making CEOSS staff available at all times.

Meanwhile in many other communities, too, various individual programmes such as family planning or tree-planting were carried out on a self-help basis, with CEOSS support but without the total engagement of a full partnership relationship.

Either way, it was the perfect mix, with CEOSS providing the expertise and the community deciding what it wanted, and both moving forward together, the ultimate beneficiary being the community itself.

As the nineties dawned, however, Sam began to feel the pressure on just how many communities CEOSS could directly assist at any one time. Money and resources limited the options. And so in 1990 CEOSS developed a new emphasis, in order to reach out to larger geographical areas through local organizations and societies already in existence.

Community development according to the partnership model, which had been going on for some time, proved effective but slow, because it relied on resident full-time CEOSS staff in the community. It also depended on a full range of programmes and activities to meet the needs of each community. Partnership development was the cornerstone of CEOSS's work, and is still an essential part of the total programme.

The new approach, however, placed greater emphasis on self-help

programmes, working through local organizations and societies
already active in the community. It was a way of reaching out to more
communities in different parts of the country, and also depended on
local leaders taking the initiative to do development.

CEOSS, however, continued to train community leaders in
various capacities, and to use their activities and services. Now every
year, in addition to CEOSS's full-time staff, more than 4,000
volunteers across the country work on CEOSS programmes in their
own communities, offering their services and skills in villages and
urban areas.

In 1991 Sam established a new department in CEOSS which
deeply touched his own heart, to deal with concerns he had prayed
about and theologically fought over in his own mind. This new
department would permit study and dialogue between Christians
and Muslims, as well as provide training opportunities for emerging
church leaders.

The tensions created by Muslim fundamentalists profoundly
concerned him, and Sam wanted a dialogue to ease the situation.
He also wanted CEOSS to look at the future needs of Egypt and
the church's role in meeting them, and to provide both a place and
an opportunity for study to be made of problems affecting the whole
nation. Sam's other main desire was to explore specific areas of
concern, such as education, with people in the government.

CEOSS continues to try to pinpoint and urgently respond to
national issues of this kind. In 1990, at a gathering of CEOSS's
council in Cairo, a cry went up for Egypt's young people, especially
with regard to their living standards and employment opportunities.
Like the government, CEOSS knows that where large-scale unemployment exists rage and violence are not far behind. It is in
these streets of fear and uncertainty that fanaticism is nurtured and
in time will rear its ugly head.

One of the chronic shortages Egypt faces with a high birthrate
is the need for housing, especially among the poor. Heeding the
call, CEOSS has recently initiated a programme of low-cost housing, beginning among garbage collector communities in Cairo. It
is pioneer work, and with no past experience to draw on only time
will tell if the housing project is successful. If it is, CEOSS will build
new houses in other poor communities.

Samuel Habib had struggled through adversity to reach the place
where he could he could now look back, see the hand of God

working in his life and quietly give thanks for the gifts he had been given, which he in turn had used to help others. It was a time not for complacency but for reflection before moving on to the next chapter of his life.

CEOSS Organizational Plan

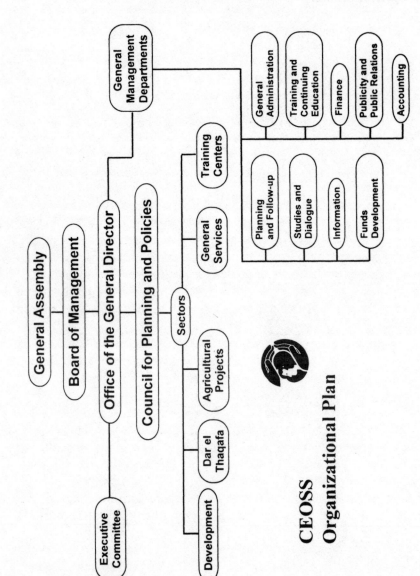

CEOSS
Organizational Plan

Chapter 5

International Connections

MISSIONARIES

For more than forty years CEOSS has reached out with helping hands into the communities and villages of millions of Egyptian men, women and children living along the River Nile, most of whose lives are blighted by poverty, ignorance and fatalism.

With headquarters in Cairo and branch offices in Minia and Alexandria, CEOSS can now cover almost the entire length of the country except for the extreme south. But the demand for its services is at times overwhelming. The need is endless; resources are not.

The task of social services in Egypt is formidable. Unlike ancient Egypt, which stood at the apex of culture and wisdom, modern Egypt faces all the problems endemic to Third World countries. Overpopulation, widespread illiteracy, low family income, high unemployment among both educated and uneducated people and chronic health hazards form the background to life in Egypt today, both in the cities and in rural areas.

From its inception CEOSS worked with foreign missionaries. In the early years they formed the backbone of Sam's outreach to the community. This has had both positive and negative results.

At certain times there were two families and three single missionaries from the Presbyterian Church (U.S.A.) working with CEOSS. At other times there were more families than single missionaries. But missionaries have worked in CEOSS in various capacities for almost thirteen years.

Then as now they worked quietly, with little fanfare, but what they did left its mark on the organization in lasting ways. One of the missionary families worked in developing leadership among community leaders, especially with pastors of rural areas. Another missionary family developed Bible study programmes for CEOSS.

Yet it was always clear that whatever roles the missionaries played, leadership in CEOSS would always remain in Egyptian hands. However, CEOSS's democratic process, which Sam had firmly established early on, always guaranteed a sharing of roles among the senior staff, both Egyptians and Americans.

Sam was the leader of CEOSS throughout the Sixties, with a staff ranging between forty and fifty. After Davida Finney's departure in 1958, Marjorie Dye and Jack Lorimer remained on the staff till 1967.

But in the mid-60s the changing political climate forced many missionaries to return to the United States. This steady trickle continued until the last of them left at the time of the Six-Day War in 1967, though some later returned. Jack Lorimer, for example, returned to teach in the seminary. But from that year on, missionaries who were still on the staff of CEOSS worked in specific roles designated by the organization.

For the most part they stayed away from field work. In the early years, CEOSS had faced a number of problems with the whole programme being stamped American because of the number of foreign missionaries working on staff. Many local communities saw this and resented it. The people wanted the programme to be run by Egyptian nationals. When they saw an American coming into a community and taking charge of a programme they often wanted no part of it.

Another problem Sam faced was having management procedures performed by American missionaries on staff. They would often find themselves confronted with laws and regulations which they did not know how to interpret, and it became increasingly difficult for them to administer delicate management situations. Newly enacted labour laws introduced by President Nasser in the Seventies were strictly enforced, for example, and the situation had to be managed very carefully.

From 1967 onward, CEOSS established a policy of only inviting expatriate partners from different countries based on their particular expertise and CEOSS's expanding needs. CEOSS continues to have expatriate partners on staff today. One is in international relations, another is a communications officer, and a third works in the publishing house, Dar El Thaqafa. A fourth couple does agricultural development. They perform their tasks in areas that do not require Arabic as a first language.

The value of expatriates is nowadays more for cultural exchanges and experience. When CEOSS invites an outside person to look critically at CEOSS occasionally, it is for the purpose of building up the organization. When problems arise, as they inevitably do, an outsider with a totally different perspective is often able to help people in the communities see other ways of doing things which in the long run can benefit them. The goal is always to better develop their programme.

CEOSS today is the largest single agency involved in community development, not only in Egypt but in the entire Middle East singlehandedly changing more lives than any other organization in the area.

From its humble beginnings it has grown into an organization with some 400 full-time staff, 200 part-timers including participation by outside doctors and nurses, and a budget of close to (US) $7 million.

A large portion of the income derives from services and sales of CEOSS-made products and books sold within Egypt. But most of the money comes in donations from supporters worldwide.

FUND-RAISING

Up until the early Seventies the Presbyterian Church (U.S.A.) provided most of the funding for CEOSS. In those days the national body of the Presbyterian Church was heavily endowed and known for its generous funding of organizations around the world.

But when the central administration of the Presbyterian Church began to experience income shortfalls from individual local churches, money for its international projects plunged dramatically. CEOSS was one of the organizations affected by the drop in giving.

Before this time CEOSS could receive no funds from other organizations or churches, especially state-funded European church bodies. They would bluntly tell Sam that because he was being funded by the Presbyterians in the United States he didn't need other funding agencies to support him. With the sudden drop in American funding, however, Sam began in the early Seventies to seek out contributions from European donors.

The Seventies proved a tough period for building relationships with new donors. Sam had to explain his work to a whole new generation of individual givers and donor agencies. But when they realized that money from the Presbyterian Church was drying up, European donors reversed their policies and began to work closely with CEOSS to provide funds. Many of the new donor agencies began sending their staff to visit Egypt on an annual basis to see what they could do to fund CEOSS's projects.

What they saw impressed them. Foreign representatives of donor organizations immediately infused CEOSS's programmes with much-needed cash and from time to time would come to see how their money was being spent. CEOSS today maintains a network of international relationships with friends all over the world.

Guests frequently come to visit CEOSS and to see the programmes.But never at any time is there the sense that they have come to run the organization or that they are decision-makers. CEOSS is one hundred percent Egyptian-owned and operated.

For CEOSS to obtain contributions and funds from abroad poses little problem as the Egyptian government also receives funds from abroad as do Muslim and other Christian organizations. The United States, for example, annually gives Egypt around $2 billion in aid.

With the Egyptian economy underdeveloped and living standards as low as they are, and with a growing population, there is a tremendous, indeed critical, need for financial support from abroad. None of CEOSS's funds however, come stamped with political agreements or with strings attached.

For a brief period, when relationships were severed with the United States in the Sixties under President Nasser, obtaining funds from abroad proved difficult. Sam made it clear to the government, through the Ministry of Social Affairs, that CEOSS would continue to seek and obtain money from abroad for its ministry to the poor. CEOSS got no argument. The funds were approved.

From time to time donor organizations sent their own auditors to Egypt to make sure funds were spent correctly. CEOSS graciously welcomed them with all due Middle Eastern hospitality. Most donors, however, were satisfied to receive CEOSS's annual audited reports.

Today, major funding comes from European countries with only a small portion coming from the United States. Contributions come from churches, organizations, individuals and foundations, and a U.S.-based organization, H.A.N.D.S. (Hands Along the Nile Development Services) Inc., established in 1989 accepts donations in the U.S. for the work of CEOSS.

But money is only a part of the partnership relationship between CEOSS and supporting organizations and individuals. More than money exchanges hands. Ideas are exchanged and opportunities afforded CEOSS staff to meet with international professionals in community development as they pass through Egypt. Useful time is spent discussing issues and problems. This has proven invaluable to Sam. Building relationships between people and agencies, Sam has learned, is oftentimes more important than money.

When donors come and study CEOSS's programmes, Sam wants them not only to be concerned about what part they can play financially to support the organization, but also to become involved in a wider dialogue about the programme, so that they can share with CEOSS staff the experiences they are having in other parts of the world. Each learns and draws from the other's experience. Sam has found over the years that these relationships are essential to the growth of CEOSS. Some donors even serve as consultants from time to time.

No other private voluntary organization in Egypt offers the comprehensive line of services available through CEOSS's development programmes.

Over the years, through the powerful and able leadership of CEOSS, hundreds of men and women have been recruited and trained to help Egypt's poor. It is not Samuel Habib's vision alone any more; it is a group of dedicated men and women working together under the umbrella of CEOSS that has and is making the difference.

The millions of lives CEOSS has touched and continues to touch and change give evidence that Samuel Habib's vision is indeed a vision of hope, a vision that has brought development and renewal to entire communities along the ever-broadening expanse of the Nile River.

Chapter 6

War and Politics

In 1964, with Nasser at the height of his power, Sam wrote a book called *The Church In A Developing Society*. It was the first and only book written by an Egyptian churchman criticizing Nasser's new socialist order. It was a courageous thing to do. Criticizing a political system embraced by a popular president and his people in a country that did not allow free speech was, to say the least, a dangerous if not reckless thing to do.

Sam was convinced, however, that the socialism Nasser called for was not the best political system for his country, and he was prepared to say so. It was a risk he was ready to take. Nasser was committed to a socialist path and, in a public speech on July 23, 1961 nationalized over 400 corporations. Some of these were private; others were cooperatives.

Back in 1954, the strong man of Egypt had ordered the arrest of the leadership of the Muslim Brotherhood in an attempt to ban their activities. This populist movement was founded in 1926 by Hassan al-Banna, an Islamic purist and moralist, largely in opposition to the secularizing nationalism of the time and the ending of the Ottoman caliphate in 1924.

The basic aim of the movement was to preserve the unity of religion and public life against Western and nationalist endeavours to separate state and religion. Nasser used the Muslim Brotherhood as a tool for winning popular support, but quickly dispensed with them once he gained power. The Brotherhood soon began to oppose Nasser once he cut them off, not giving them the share of power they had been hoping for. Nasser, in turn, now saw them as a threat and wanted them out of the way.

Sam's book, published and sold by Dar El Thaqafa, contained a critical analysis of Marxist socialism, and Arab socialism in particular. His criticisms were forthright and brought quick retaliation from the small but flourishing Communist Party in Egypt (later absorbed into the Nasserist regime). Criticism pushed the book up the sales chart and around 2,000 copies were snapped up immediately in bookshops around the country.

Predictably, the book came to the attention of government officials. Sam was paid a visit by Egypt's secret police and interrogated for some time about his intentions and political motives. Sam responded by saying that he wrote what he did as a loyal Egyptian out of concern for his country. He wanted to see Egypt move forward with major reforms.

Sam argued that not every rich man in Egypt was a capitalist bent on doing evil and hurting his labourers. Many were doing a decent job serving their country. Sam then went on to argue that a company formed by the people and supported by the government would not necessarily be successful, as the people in time wouldn't care whether the company was productive or not. There was no incentive for its success, no profit motive.

Sam's book examined the theological implications of socialism, arguing that the individual was ultimately responsible to God alone for the stewardship of what he had been given. In God's economy employers were called upon to treat their employees with justice and equity and employees should give the best they had to their employers. Everyone in the end would profit. Private enterprise was not in and of itself evil, though it could be used for excessive personal gain and greed.

The book also focused on the church's role during this period, an issue which some of Sam's friends considered very radical. A number of great preachers in Egypt at the time were advocating Christian socialism using various Biblical texts in support of their sermons. They justified their political point of view by referring to verses in the book of Acts where disciples in the early church voluntarily gave the apostles their properties.

Sam criticized the misuse of these New Testament texts and the socialist twist given to them by these preachers, roundly condemning Marxist socialism as it was being practised in Egypt. The state, in this instance, was forcibly seizing money and appropriating properties from ordinary people by government decree.

In the New Testament, Sam argued, newly converted Christian disciples gave voluntarily of their properties and money without coercion, a different matter altogether.

Sam contended vigorously against any notion of 'Christian' socialism in the political or religious sense, arguing that it could not be found in the Bible. The Bible, he said, had no economic systems. The Bible's concern is for the poor. The problem with the Marxist's system was in giving the power and riches to a small minority of people using the political order to make the poor poorer. He argued, moreover, that Marxist socialism was neither good politics nor good economics. At the same time he pointed out the limitations, indeed evils, of unbridled capitalism, and said the priority should always be to serve the poor. There is no one economic system which is perfect for this. We must, he said, take the best of whatever system we can find and use it to benefit the poor.

The truth, Sam knew, was that most of these preachers were trying to please the government and make Marxist socialism fit the Bible at the same time. But it was at the expense of truth, and Sam would not tolerate that. So Sam stood his ground, adding to his police interrogators that what he had written could be accepted by any Muslim as loyal to Islam as he was faithful to Christianity.

The secret police took their statements and departed. As they left they told Sam that a report would be given to His Excellency the Minister of the Interior for further action. Happily, nothing more was heard about the matter. The concerns the secret police raised about Sam's political aspirations, like Marxist socialism itself, simply died away.

On June 6, 1967 war broke out between Egypt and Israel. It was the third of four Arab wars with Israel and it proved disastrous. At the time, Sam was flying to Toronto, Canada for a week's preaching in the United Church of Canada at the denomination's invitation.

He had flown in from New York on June 3, with a blazing headline in the *New York Times* stating that the American Embassy in Egypt was requesting all American citizens leave the country. Sam knew that war was imminent.

When he arrived at the airport he told his waiting host that he was sorry, but he could not stay and must return home immediately, as war between his country and Israel was inevitable. His host, visibly upset, showed Sam newspaper announcements about his forthcoming preaching and told him radio broadcasts were already going out on the airwaves every hour inviting people to come and hear him. Sam was clearly in an awkward situation. He did not want to offend his host, yet at the same time he knew he had to be back in Egypt to stand alongside his people as they went to war.

Sam compromised. He told his host that he would preach only on Sunday morning and then make a tape recording for the evening service. His host agreed. At the hotel that night he got a call from the pastor urging him to speak directly to the Middle East situation next morning in church. As the two men spoke, Sam listened with a heavy heart to radio broadcasts announcing that Nasser had ordered United Nations troops away from the borders separating Israel and Egypt and out of the Gulf of Aqaba.

On Sunday morning Sam preached from the pulpit on the political situation in the Middle East. It was one of the hardest and emotionally draining sermons he had ever preached. He later made a recording for the evening service and was then rushed to the airport. The door of the airliner was already locked and the plane about to leave its bay when airline officials saw Sam dashing through the terminal towards the aircraft. Instinctively they signalled the captain and brought the plane to a halt. Officials opened the door and let Sam on board. He sank into his seat with the weight of the world, or at least the Middle East, on his shoulders, and arrived back in Egypt just as war was declared. His was the last commercial jet allowed to land at Cairo's international airport before it closed.

A black-out was declared on the first day of the war and everyone gathered around their radios to listen to the war's progress. The nation was psyched for victory. Sam was living in Minia with his family at the time, though he still retained his office in Cairo. He gathered his family and the CEOSS staff around him to wait out the war.

Sam told his staff they could stop work, and that they would receive their salaries regardless of what was going on, or the outcome of the war. He told them that when the war was over they would begin again and set about correcting things.

Five days later the war ended. The Egyptian army was routed by the Israelis and resoundingly defeated on all fronts. It was a period of national shame. The defeat was a devastating blow to Egyptian morale and pride, and the results were serious in all aspects of Egyptian life economically, spiritually and politically. The war, Sam later learned, was lost in the first three hours, with the air force and military effectively neutralized by the Israelis.

The United States brokered the peace. Nasser, who had been in power for eighteen years and had overseen Egypt's growth into a great country, was now faced with his nation's destruction and his own personal humiliation. He died in 1970 a defeated man.

For Sam and CEOSS it was time now to build up national confidence again. The process would be slow. He waited a month and then called his staff back to work. Demoralized and saddened, they returned.

After the June 1967 War all American Presbyterian missionaries left Egypt. The decision came from the Presbyterian Church in the United States. The advice it gave its missionaries in Egypt was that they should leave their jobs immediately and return to the United States for good. Missionaries returned home to consult with their churches, and the churches accepted their return not knowing what the future was going to be. It would now be up to the Synod of the Nile to reconsider their task and their needs, and to request those missionaries they wanted back.

A year later, a consultation took place between the Presbyterian Church (U.S.A.) and the Synod of the Nile to map out strategies for the future, and to strengthen the partnership relationship between the two churches in preparation for whatever the future held.

A number of missionaries returned to Egypt in response to the expressed needs of the Egyptian Church. Professors returned to teach in the seminaries, and educators were hired for the School Board and to help meet Egypt's growing need for trained teachers.

It was the dawn of a new day. Relationships from now on would be determined by the leaders and heads of Egypt's Evangelical Church rather than by the dictates of a foreign church board. Future relationships would revolve around the concept of partnership. The old colonial mentality was now a thing of the past.

While Sam had no intention of ever allowing CEOSS to become politicized, nor was it his intention to take sides in political battles or affirm one political party over another, he did write an editorial on the 1967 war in his magazine Risalet Al-Noor (Message of Light). The magazine was published by CEOSS for new literates and Egypt's more simple readers. It was not aimed at politically sophisticated thinkers.

Sam saw that the Egyptian people needed to be encouraged, and through his magazine he sought to do just that. The purpose of his column was to provide moral support for the people and to boost their morale, now at an all-time low in their political history. The main thrust of the article was that even in defeat it was still possible to stand again on one's feet as a nation and build a better future.

Prior to this, in 1964, Sam published a new magazine called *Agnahet Al-Nasoor* (Wings of the Eagles), directed towards church leaders. The magazine was jointly owned and edited with his friends Dr. Fayez Faris, Dr. Menis Abdel-Noor and the Rev. Amir Gayyed, who later died during a kidney transplant operation. At the time both Menis Abdel-Noor and Amir Gayyed were working in senior positions with CEOSS.

The four of them established the theological magazine for the purpose of giving themselves the freedom to air issues relevant to Egypt's situation and needs and to provide future direction for the church. It was registered with the government and became an officially recognized magazine among the churches and an important arm in the leadership of the church. Over time the magazine became more ecumenical, inviting both Orthodox and Catholic leaders to participate and be on its board.

Agnahet Al-Nasoor dealt mostly with current affairs, societal concerns, theology and church issues analyzed from the perspective of Scripture. One of its real concerns was to relate theology to society and life and to give more depth to the church's pronouncements. Each of the four editors, Amir, Menis, Fayez and Sam, was responsible for one department, and the departments were very carefully chosen. Sam was responsible for the department on science and religion; Fayez presided over the department of theology and doctrine; Menis took responsibility for Biblical studies and Biblical issues; and Amir reflected on general problems that youth were facing in the church. Over the course of time their responsibilities changed, but the magazine remained a rich source of interest and reflection for all church leaders in Egypt.

As time passed the four men got busier with their respective duties. Menis and Amir both received calls to large pastorates in Cairo and withdrew from CEOSS.

Menis became pastor of Qasr El Dubbara Church, the largest Evangelical Church in Egypt, while Amir went off to the U.S. to study, and on his return became pastor of Faggala Evangelical Church in another quarter of Cairo; he later passed away.

The magazine was left to other writers. As a result the standard of articles slowly dropped, forcing the remaining three editors to come together again in 1992 to re-evaluate the magazine and look at its future. More than twenty clergy including Orthodox, Catholic and Protestant leaders met at the Horriya Hotel in Cairo to discuss the magazine's future, and moves were made to restructure it. A new board was set up, a new policy was formulated and a new editor was chosen. It was now truly ecumenical.

In September 1967, Sam was invited to the first International Christian Publishers' Seminar in Stony Point, New York, led by Dr. Marion Van Horne and Frederick Rex of 'Lit-Lit', the literacy department of the NCCC. Marion and Frederick, both NCCC staffers had contributed a great deal over the years to the success of CEOSS's literacy work. They had several times helped with the training of writers for new literates in Egypt, including a Middle East-wide workshop at Fairhaven, Alexandria, in northern Egypt back in 1958.

Sam was the only person from Egypt at the Stony Point seminar, in fact the only person from the whole Middle East among a group of thirty-five men and women to attend.

He was able to share what he had learned in the course of his work as a Christian publisher in the Middle East, and his presence strengthened the resolve of publishers in other Third World countries to overcome the hurdles they faced publishing Christian literature. While Sam was able to share the joys and sorrows of publishing Christian literature in a predominantly Muslim country, by sharing and learning from the experiences of others, he too gained strength and insight to continue with his own agenda. Peace and justice were at the heart of his commitment.

After the death of Nasser in 1970, Anwar Sadat became Egypt's president, a man Sam very much appreciated and admired. A new political era had dawned for the Egyptian people. In 1974 Sadat established a new international open-door economic policy, inviting foreign investment in Egypt. After years of economic deprivation under Nasser, the presence of new money and the sight of Western products flooding the market gave Egyptians new hope.

Sadat also began releasing Muslim Brotherhood prisoners Nasser had put in jail. Because of his open-door economic policy, those members of the Brotherhood who had fled to neighbouring Arab states during the 1950s and 1960s to avoid persecution and had made their fortunes there now returned to Egypt and invested their money in Egypt's ailing economy.

Not wanting to upset this newly-returned wealthy middle class,

Sadat immediately set about proving he was a true follower of Islam, adopting Islamic discourse and even amending the Constitution to say that the Shari'a, or Islamic law was a principle source of Egyptian legislation. And he allowed both education and the mass media to be used as channels for the Muslim religion.

At first people didn't realize just how clever Sadat was, and he was content to let them think that he was just a fool who couldn't care less about anything but his own image. In fact, people were supposed to think that Sadat's words and actions meant nothing. He certainly wanted it that way when he launched the 1973 October War.

He had repeatedly told the people he was going to war with Israel, but nobody really believed him, yet that is precisely what happened. When he declared war in 1973 it caused a major shift in the thinking of the Egyptian people. Sadat, the 'political clown', now became a national leader and hero.

The Egyptian army had crossed the Suez Canal and regained part of the Sinai Peninsula, as Sadat had promised, when Egypt called first for peace and the United States intervened to negotiate a peace at the last moment.

Sadat was nevertheless appreciated for the way he did what he had done. The people regained their national pride and their morale was lifted. Once again they began to respect their place in history and in the international community.

People began to respect Sadat. When he began negotiations for peace with Israel, which ended bloodshed between the Jewish state and its largest Arab neighbour, Sam personally appreciated him even more, and wanted to honour Sadat by arranging for him to be given an honourary doctor's degree, as an expression of gratitude from the Church in Egypt.

The peace accords signed by Israeli Prime Minister Menachem Begin, U.S. President Jimmy Carter and Anwar Sadat opened the door to the first honest attempt at peace in the Middle East, and this struck a deep chord in the Protestant leader. It was a breakthrough in ways that could not have been imagined. No one could have foreseen that twenty years later a new young United States president, a Palestinian leader and an Israeli Prime Minister would again shake hands to usher in a new era of peace.

Sam began looking for an American university or college that would confer a doctorate on Sadat, but he had a difficult time locating one that would go along with the idea. Everybody would say to him: if we give an honorary doctor's degree to Sadat, we must give one to Begin as well. To find a university or a college that would bestow honours on Sadat, and yet wouldn't press the issue about Begin, was extremely difficult.

It wasn't that Sam was not interested in honouring Menachem Begin; he just felt it wasn't his job. He argued that he was an Egyptian and what he was doing, he was doing for Sadat and Egypt. It was up to others to concern themselves with Begin and Israel. It was not his business to intervene for a prime minister of another country.

Sam finally found Muskingham College, a liberal arts school in Ohio, and its president Dr. Arthur DeJung, who was willing to support the idea. Sam invited Dr. DeJung to Egypt to make the special presentation, because Sam wanted it known and heard throughout Egypt that the United States admired Sadat, and that the Egyptian Church admired Sadat and appreciated his diplomatic efforts.

Sam felt that what Sadat had done was prophetic. It was good not only for Egypt but for the whole Arab world as well. The honorary doctorate was a statement to the Palestinian people that Samuel Habib cared for and thought about them. As Sam was President of the Protestant Churches of Egypt, the doctorate was given on behalf of the Protestant community. It was a red letter day in Samuel Habib's life.

The doctorate was conferred on Sadat on March 13, 1980 in the auditorium of the Ramses College for Girls in Cairo. Sadat delegated Mr. Mustafa Kamal Helmi, the most senior minister in his cabinet and Minister of Education, later chairman of the Shura Council (upper chamber of parliament), to represent him for the occasion and to receive the degree on his behalf.

The next day Sadat received Sam and the American delegation, which included a group of international church leaders, into his home at Qanater (Barrages), north of Cairo.

The group included Dr. Donald Black and Dr. Victor Makari from the Presbyterian Church (U.S.A.), Dr. Jack Lorimer, Dr. DeJung and Dr. Hans Bootsma from the Dutch Reformed Church in the Netherlands.

Sam never met Nasser, but he had encountered Sadat before, and met with him on several occasions after that. Years later, following the death of Sadat, Samuel Habib met a number of times with President Hosni Mubarak. At the meeting with Sadat, Dr. DeJung presented the Egyptian president with the gift of an ancient book given by a member of the United States Congress and board member of Muskingham College.

The occasion also gave Sam an opportunity to encourage Sadat in a project that he, Sadat, wanted to establish in Egypt, namely to construct a temple, a church and a mosque in one building overlooking the Sinai hills.

To help start the project, Sam offered Sadat a special contribution of $15,000 which he had collected from the Dutch Reformed Church in the Netherlands and the Presbyterian Church (U.S.A.) exclusively for this purpose. Sam gave Sadat the cheque and told the president he thought the project was extremely important as a signal of religious peace, if not unity, in the Arab world. As the venture had not yet begun, Sam hoped it would be used as seed money to get the project started. Sadat looked at Sam and said: 'You know, I wanted the government to pay for it, but the way you are doing it is much better. It is better that the people pay for it, and in this way we will cultivate love among the three religions within our country. I'll do it the way you suggest.' Sadly, the temple/mosque/church complex never materialized. Sadat was assassinated a year later in 1981 by a Muslim fanatic within a military unit in a passing victory parade. The idea, and the money, disappeared with Sadat's death.

On October 6, 1980 Sam was asked by a representative of Sadat to become a founding member of the Association of Islamic and Arab Peoples. Under Sadat, because of the Camp David treaty, the League of Arab Nations withdrew its headquarters from Egypt and moved to Tunisia. Sadat's part in the signing of the Camp David accords had angered a number of Arab nations, and as a result they broke diplomatic ties with Egypt. Sadat, in response, established a counter-organization, the Association for the Islamic and Arab Peoples, and chose sixty people to be its founding members. Sam was one of them.

Sam accepted the position because it included both Islamic and Arab peoples, and so by definition non-Islamic people in the Arab world. By including everyone – Christian and Muslim alike Sadat sought to reach out to all Arab peoples and nations, regardless of nationality and religion. Of the sixty founding members five were

Christians. Most of the Arab countries were represented by leading figures in the community, but few government heads or politicians attended.

President Sadat headed and chaired the council himself. Sam attended all the meetings. While the organization had no power to make political changes, it did signal an openness and awareness in the Arab world that their inward-looking attitudes and hatred served no good purpose. The way of peace was the way of the future. The organization continued until the presidency of Hosni Mubarak. Later, when the headquarters of the Arab League returned to Egypt from Tunisia, the association ceased to exist.

Under Sadat, Nasser's experiment with Arab socialism in Egypt crumbled. The new president's open-door economic policy brought much-needed foreign investment. The West began to trade with and, cautiously, invest in Egypt. Better relationships were established between Egypt and the United States.

Under Nasser, Sam like almost everybody else had occasionally experienced harassment from the government. When Nasser broke diplomatic ties with the United States, Sam was approached by a government official and asked if he had any relationship with the U.S. Sam replied that he had. The questioner responded that Egypt had cut diplomatic ties with the United States and so should Sam.

Sam said his relationship with the United States was not diplomatic or political in nature but church-related. He argued that if Egypt was in trouble with the Soviet Union one would not expect Muslim leaders to cut their ties with Muslims in that country. In the same way he would not cut his ties with the churches in the United States or Europe or anywhere else in the world.

A nation could cut its diplomatic ties with another country without that automatically meaning cutting commercial and other ties. Other relationships, including religious alliances, would always continue and never be destroyed whatever the politicians might do. CEOSS always remained above the political fray, even though it was deeply affected by the decisions politicians made. The organization would always act as a lightning rod, upholding the word of justice and righteousness, whoever was in power.

In 1982, two years after Sadat had received his doctorate, Muskingham College conferred an honorary doctorate on Sam too. The degree was awarded for his support of peace in the Middle East and for his unique role in the social development of Egypt through the establishment of CEOSS. It was his first international honour.

On May 19, 1984, however, Sam earned a full doctorate in his own right, with a Doctor of Ministry (D.Min.) degree from San Francisco Theological Seminary in California.

On September 13, 1990 the National Council of Churches of Christ in the United States honoured him as one of three world leaders in literacy. The honour was conferred on him during United Nations International Literacy Year, and Sam's name was placed on the honour roll of the NCCC in New York City.

Because of his growing stature in the Egyptian community, Samuel Habib was elected in 1991 to be President of the Fellowship of Middle East Evangelical Churches. The Fellowship provided yet another forum for growing relationships among Evangelicals, bringing them together from across the Middle East to work for justice and peace in the region.

These honours for Sam were fitting accolades for a life spent in service for his Lord and Master. But more, much more, was still waiting to be done.

Chapter 7

A Vision for the Church

From his earliest memories Sam Habib had a vision of the church's mission, and it was significantly more than what he saw being carried out in Egypt.

He had studied hard, earned his degrees and struggled deeply with the conventional wisdom that the church was living and carrying out its mission to the fullest extent possible. From his perspective the church fell far short of its potential and capabilities. The churches could do more, much more.

Sam saw the churches as too ingrown and preoccupied with their own immediate concerns, their own survival, and very self-serving.

The church's task was and is to preach a clear apostolic and biblical message calling people to repentance and faith in Jesus Christ. Yet at the same time it could not ignore its other calling, to serve the world as Jesus did. The church, then, had a dual responsibility: to announce the Good News of salvation in Jesus Christ, and to act as an agency of change and development in people's lives.

The church, if it was to be holistic, had to identify with people in their present circumstances, especially the poor, the disabled and the marginalized, empowering them to realize their full potential in this life and not simply wait around for pie in the sky when they died.

This was not to make light of the biblical doctrine of redemption. The world was fallen, that was true. Sin had entered in, and the consequences of man's fallenness were evident all around him and in all he touched. Yet, in Christ's redemption, salvation was possible not only for people's souls but also for their bodies, the environment and the communities they lived in. Transformation of the whole cosmos was now possible because of Christ's death and resurrection. This was part of the gospel's declaration of Good News.

In the Incarnation, God identified with humanity in the person of Jesus Christ and stooped to reveal himself, being born in a manger, the condition of which was not unlike tens of thousands of village dwellings in Egypt. In redemption Jesus went to a cross and died for the world's sin and rebellion against God. Forgiveness and healing have now become possible, and this in effect means that substantial healing of the whole human condition is now reasonable to expect.

Mind, body and spirit, the environment, the land people lived on, clean water, healthy babies, overcoming fear and shattering superstitions . . . all these things were now at least possible. Luke 4:18–19 was now a realization.

Jesus had been anointed to preach the gospel to the poor, to proclaim release to the captives and recovery of sight to the blind, to set free the downtrodden and to proclaim the favourable year of the Lord.

One could not throw up one's hands and fatalistically declare that the whole world was going downhill, and the sooner it self-destructed the quicker would be the return of Christ. That was to disobey the will and intention of a loving God who wanted to see his people, many of whom lived in abject poverty, lifted out of their wretched condition.

Sam Habib argued that the church should not only cry out against injustice in the world but also act positively in bringing about justice and reconciliation for people where they lived. To bring a message of redemption and hope meant not only salvation for the life to come, but real permanent change in this life that demonstrated the message of Jesus's empowerment in people's daily lives.

In Jesus's teaching Sam Habib saw a message of holistic living. He wanted people to trust Jesus Christ as Saviour and Lord and be in a right relationship with God. At the same time he wanted people to be in a right relationship with each other and with the broader community.

The former message could be preached; the latter had to be lived out. God's love had to be made real in and through Christians reaching out to their neighbours. Anything less was not to fulfil the commandment of loving one's neighbour as oneself.

CEOSS was bringing the love of Christ to a hurting and broken world. When one looks into the faces of those who work for CEOSS, one sees the love of Jesus, and that is as it should be. But how could the church in Egypt say it loved God and ignore the poverty of millions around it? The inconsistencies stared Sam Habib in the face and deeply troubled him.

Sam now straddled a fence of his own making. On one side he had a foot firmly planted in the soil of the church as head of the Protestant community in Egypt, and on the other side he had a foot firmly planted in the soil of Egypt as General Director of CEOSS, the largest development agency serving the poor in the Middle East.

Sam saw the church's responsibility and task as being directed towards the community and not simply focusing exclusively on its own agenda contained within its own four walls. Its life and worship had to spill out onto the streets and affect the lives of everyone it touched. The church had to take a greater and more visible responsibility towards the larger community in which it had been planted. Sam Habib saw the need for church members to become more active and responsible as members of the wider community.

He began to write about what he saw and what touched his heart. From the very first book he wrote in seminary in 1947, on *Prayer*, till 1992, more than fifty titles poured from his pen.

He wrote a series of books on the Church and State, on the Church and Development, and on Church Management, and a critical assessment of Liberation Theology, one of the few books in Arabic on the subject.

He wrote hundreds of magazine articles addressing every conceivable subject. They quickly found their way onto the streets and into bookshops, churches and villages. The books and articles became part of the basis of thought and action of CEOSS and for many social service agencies springing up in Egypt.

When Liberation Theology was hailed as the new theology for the poor and advocated by the church in Latin America, Samuel Habib found himself seriously reflecting on this new theological approach. The term itself, he believed, was being wrongly used. The premise of Liberation Theology was that society set the agenda for the church and then use Scripture to defend it. Sam saw this approach as fundamentally flawed.

From Sam's perspective this was putting the proverbial cart before the horse. The church has a responsibility towards society, but theology begins first with the word of God and then reflects back to the community. Jesus's preferential option for the poor did not negate, in Sam's mind, the need for people to be brought out of their poverty and for the church to be actively involved in that process. At the same time, the church could not abrogate its responsibility to present the gospel clearly and unambiguously and see its message of faith heeded and obeyed.

The churches in Egypt, in all their three branches, are by and large conservative, with a handful of fundamentalists among them.

Christian fundamentalists in Egypt are non-violent, pietistic and take an indirect approach to any confrontation with the state or with other religious groups. They also tend towards a theology that condemns the world to the Devil except for a few souls being snatched from the flames of Hell. They seem to have no understanding of Christ's redemption of the whole earth, God's concern for the poor and the real possibility of change in this life. This theology, for Sam, was too short-sighted and did not proclaim the whole counsel of God.

Egyptian Muslims, too, tend to be rather conservative. Almost all Muslims in Egypt belong to the Sunni branch of Islam (unlike the Shi'ites of Iran). Large numbers regularly observe daily prayers, Friday mosque attendance and the Ramadan fast; and in recent years growing numbers of young Egyptian women have taken to wearing the veil or at least a large headscarf. They, too, have their fundamentalists.

The underlying reasons for both Christian and Muslim fundamentalism are psychological and sociological. The mentality behind both of them is much the same, and both tend to depend on various forms of intimidation. Fundamentalists on neither side will change their attitudes unless they experience healing in their understanding first of themselves and then of others and of the community at large.

Yet some fundamentalists, including Muslims though not the militants among them, see the possibility of dialogue and co-operation.

In coming to terms with Egypt's growing social problems, CEOSS demonstrates to them that they share a common humanity and a desire to bring about justice non-violently for the poor. In doing this, CEOSS finds itself accepted by many Muslims as well as Christians, including fundamentalists.

With the government's pronouncement that it will no longer be a hiring agency for every graduate coming out of high school and university, and with fewer private sector jobs on the horizon, unemployment is rapidly increasing in Egypt. Education and health services are also deteriorating, and Muslim militants use these things to win support for their anti-government campaign, because of the Government's inaction and inability to assist poor people and their families. The ultimate end of the radicals' campaign against government corruption is to topple the secular government and impose strict Islamic rule in the country.

While the state is not in any real imminent danger of collapsing as a result of militant violence, the psychological impact is taking its toll not only on tourism, and with it the economy, but also on the Egyptian people themselves. Violence in Egypt is not being eliminated, despite a heavy government clampdown. Hundreds of extremists and policemen have died, along with a number of civilians.

The terrorists themselves are only a small part of a much larger marginalized generation.

Their slogan, 'Islam is the solution', puts fear into ordinary Muslims who want peaceful change and fear what violence will do to their lives. The country is in profound transition, with the final outcome not yet in sight.

CEOSS, however, is in a position to serve Muslim communities and reach out to moderate Muslims, through dialogue and education. Open-minded Muslims are capable of separating out propaganda from legitimate Islamic thought.

Samuel Habib sees in the Evangelical Church in Egypt the possibility of faith and development being brought together in everyday life, thereby reducing the tensions among fundamentalists who see their personal and social lives as lacking dignity and meaning. If the people's needs can be met, at least at the economic and social level, then real hope for peace is possible.

For centuries the ancient Christian churches of Egypt were caught up in rituals and traditions that stifled their social outreach. When the Presbyterian and Anglican churches first came to Egypt in the 19th century, they helped to breathe new life into the country's staid religious apparatus. Today many Christian clerics are beginning to take note of their country's problems and actively address them.

While CEOSS was the first organization to do comprehensive development work among the 'garbage people' of Cairo, bringing new programmes of hygiene, cleanliness and sanitation, the Catholic church has long been active among such communities. Today the Coptic Orthodox Church can also be found working with these people.

The garbage people, Christian and Muslim, perform a very necessary service in Cairo. They alone pick up the waste of the city centre and suburbs, recycle and sell what they can and burn the rest. They have always lived, amidst their garbage and their animals, in the most appalling conditions, but thanks to the work of the churches and CEOSS there is now real hope for the next generation.

For the most part, though, Protestant churches have failed to see social work as a legitimate calling for them, and stand guilty of the same inaction as many of the ancient churches.

Catholics in Egypt had, for more than a century, concentrated their efforts in the area of education, establishing high-quality schools throughout the country. They built monasteries in the heart of communities that enabled the monks or nuns to retreat from the world and yet step back into the world as God called them. Today they have broadened their activities into a wide range of social and pastoral work.

Coptic Orthodox monasteries, established by monks in desert areas, had a different calling. They were isolated from society and adopted a very different attitude towards the world at large. Nowadays, the Orthodox Church shows great concern for Bible reading and exposition, and runs some very progressive Sunday Schools, youth groups and women's organizations.

Today there are some 900 Protestant congregations in Egypt, many of which are experiencing renewal and revival. Many of them have a vigorous programme of spiritual nurture for young people, and include training for women and children in basic programmes for daily living. The spiritual fire they have lit has been picked up by the Orthodox churches, and the result has been a renewed interest by both groups in working together.

Up until the 1940s denominations and churches expended a lot of energy attacking one another and writing polemics against each other's doctrinal positions. Today the theological climate is gradually improving. Clergy and laity can often be seen sitting down and talking with one another, demonstrating a friendliness they have never experienced before. Christians of Protestant, Orthodox and Catholic persuasions are also building stronger relationships and working together as never before.

Relationships between the Evangelical and Catholic churches in Egypt, which were strong through the years, are growing stronger, and they now openly support each other. Relationships between the Coptic Orthodox and Evangelical churches have also been growing, and while there have been ups and downs in the past they are closer today than they have ever been before. Now they can often be found sitting down in dialogue together at both lay and clergy levels and even higher up the hierarchy.

Among the laity there is not only talk but activity as well. A large number of inter-church activities are taking place at the denominational level. There is a new-found respect for one another's positions even though agreement on some theological issues is impossible.

Samuel Habib views it as deeply significant that, regardless of denominational loyalties, Christians of all persuasions are talking to each other and forming strong relationships in their everyday lives, both in the workplace and as they live together in the same apartment complexes.

Meanwhile thousands of Christians enjoy close relationships with Muslims and vice versa. In some places there is growing friendliness and increasing unanimity between the two groups. Islamic extremists have succeeded in pushing the two groups together.

In the mid-Sixties Sam Habib established a first in ecumenical relations, opening the door to joint study programmes and action among Protestant, Catholic and Orthodox leaders. He called a meeting of church leaders, the first of its kind ever to be held in the religious life and history of Egypt.

Samuel Habib, representing the Evangelical and Protestant churches in Egypt, met together with Bishop Samuel of the Orthodox church and Pere Henry Ayrout, a Jesuit leader in the Egyptian Catholic Church. Father Ayrout was deeply involved in rural work and had established the Catholic Society for Upper Egypt Schools. Bishop Samuel held the position of bishop for ecumenical and social services in the Coptic Orthodox Church. Sam, of course, was the general director of CEOSS. Together the three men sat down on a series of occasions, at various locations in Cairo and Minia, and sought to find ways in which they could co-operate together.

After much discussion it was felt that the family and issues surrounding family life were the biggest single concern drawing them together, and so they decided to hold a number of seminars under the general title of The Christian Rural Conference.

The seminars were held in Minia and each church took turns at hosting the event. A committee was formed to run the programme, drawn from people who lived in Minia as well as Cairo and Assiut. Sam saw this as a practical way for the churches to work together collaboratively in areas that did not require doctrinal agreement, avoiding the kinds of issue that might otherwise have separated them.

This significantly increased Sam's prominence and standing within the Egyptian Christian community, and his activities were now being highly regarded. His stature within the Evangelical Church ranked him as an outstanding next- generation leader.

In 1965 he was unanimously elected General Secretary of the Synod of the Nile of the Evangelical Church of Egypt. Over the next 12 years he was unanimously re-elected three more times to further four-year terms in the position. This in itself was an exception to the rules. The Synod's regulations stated that a general secretary could serve only two terms. A special exception was made for Samuel Habib. He had earned it.

As General Secretary, Sam now sought to modernize the Synod. This caused resentment among some of the church leaders. Over the years, it had become customary for the General Secretary of the Synod to read out the minutes of the previous year's meeting from his own copious hand-written notes, after which the entire Synod of 150 pastors, representing all the Evangelical churches in Egypt would vote on them.

This amateurish approach to synod business frustrated Sam. He decided to get the reports and minutes printed up and distributed to each member of the Synod well before the annual meeting took place. Members would no longer have to vote from memory. Sam then established an office as the General Secretariat of the Synod and employed a young woman as a secretary.

All of this enraged some of the more traditional and staid members of the Synod, who charged Sam with going against tradition and spending money unnecessarily on printing and staff. In truth, the changes he was making clearly benefited everyone, and Sam was prepared to withstand petty envy and resentments. It took three years for everyone to accept the changes he proposed, but he was determined that the denomination's business would be done in a proper professional manner, reflecting the times in which it lived as well as allowing for future planning. His hope was that the Synod would become a prophetic voice in the community.

Meanwhile, Sam was also nominated to be chairman of the Church's Council on Service and Development. His abilities and leadership qualities again got him re-elected unanimously to that position for a total of four terms, a period of 16 years.

A major portion of his responsibility on this council was to raise funds locally and from abroad for church-related projects in Egypt, as well as to provide education in development.

But the combination of his various roles began to weigh heavily on him. Trying to maintain the right balance was more than he could humanly do. As chairman of the council he insisted on replacing himself. He sought and found someone he could train to take over his position as chairman, and even though it was an elected position the council agreed.

In another move to relieve himself of some of the duties he was performing during his last term as General Secretary of the Synod, Sam opened an office for the assistant general secretary and arranged for him to have a secretary. Sam then made sure that all the secretaries of the church's various presbyteries and councils were made responsible to the new man, and that the papers they produced went to his assistant rather than to himself.

Samuel Habib's church leadership abilities and development work through CEOSS were now being recognized by the broader international Christian community outside of Egypt, and he was chosen to be a member of the Association for Christian Literature Development (ACLD), a body that worked closely with the World Council of Churches. It was later dissolved and replaced by the World Association for Christian Communication (WACC), the new communication arm of the WCC.

WACC encompassed not only literature but also radio, TV and the press, whereas the ACLD had focused almost exclusively on literature and literacy. Sam was a member of WACC for eleven years.

Though independent of the WCC, the ACLD brought Sam into contact with several organizations doing literature and literacy work around the world. The group met yearly in different countries, and this afforded Sam the opportunity to touch base with churches in those countries. He was thus able to review what was going on in the broader Christian community and current thinking among church leaders.

In 1976 he was elected, for a seven-year term, as vice-president of the World Alliance of Reformed Churches (WARC), and then for another seven years as a member of the executive committee.

Between 1971 and 1985 Sam was an appointed member of the WCC Commission on Inter-Church Aid, Refugee and World Service (CICARWS), and in this post he travelled extensively, evaluating church aid and refugee organizations around the world. It also gave him the opportunity to study political, social and religious issues as they related to the Middle East, and to share the information with WCC members.

CICARWS afforded Sam the opportunity to think globally yet bring back ideas with which CEOSS could act locally. It also gave him a chance to see how churches dealt with problems in their own context. Above all, it gave Samuel Habib, a man steeped in Arab culture and with a deep Christian faith, broad insights into how other countries dealt with complex theological and development problems. It then gave him a platform from which to pronounce on issues of the day with great authority.

In 1991, at the World Council of Churches' meeting in Canberra, Australia, Sam was chosen as a member of the Commission on Church in Mission: Health, Education and Witness and was a member of its executive committee. This gave him an unprecedented opportunity both to listen and to share his own experiences in Egypt with the wider church community. It also allowed him to dialogue with others on pressing issues of mission and evangelism, and the North-South polarities relating to rich and poor, including the obligations of the former to the latter. Sam felt it was an obligation of the rich nations to stand alongside the poor and to give of their abundance, not in a paternalistic manner or with strings attached, but simply because it was the right thing to do. There was no room now in the global village for money and food to be used politically to manipulate people or to put a stranglehold on people for political ends. Nor should food be used as an evangelistic tool to make Christian converts, he believed. Christian giving, and the proclamation of Christ, should not come with strings attached. Sam said it was incumbent on rich churches in the West to give of their wealth to their poorer brethren in the Two-Thirds world because both the gospels and the early church, through its apostles, demanded this of them, with Jesus setting the example.

The WCC meeting also afforded Sam ample opportunity to explain the Arab cause to world Christian leaders, and in several meetings he was able to interpret the whole Middle East situation and assert the right of Palestinians to have a piece of land to call their own.

In January 1980 tragedy struck. Sam's longstanding friend and confidant the Rev. Elias Maqar, president of the Protestant Churches of Egypt, suddenly died. The two men had worked together in a variety of ways over the years, and his death was a significant personal loss to Sam as well as a blow to the Christian community.

His death also now left a vacancy at the head of the Protestant Church Council. With no dissent Samuel Habib, by now a seasoned churchman and elder statesman, was nominated and elected the new president of the Protestant Churches in Egypt on March 26, 1980. It was a singular honour, but for a man who had worked so hard for his people it was by any standards well deserved.

The Protestant Church Council, an umbrella organization acting as a kind of federation for the Protestant Churches in Egypt, draws together some sixteen denominations, including Presbyterians, Anglicans, Methodists, Baptists, Brethren, Pentecostalists and Assemblies of God, in all their various branches. By far and away the largest single denomination among them is the Evangelical (Presbyterian) Church, which has roughly 300 congregations across Egypt.

No new Protestant denomination can be established in Egypt without the approval of this Council, and while each denomination is autonomous there are certain matters within the church as a whole and in ecumenical, that have to be carried out by the council.

The body is recognized and approved by the government, and Samuel Habib's new role was also an officially recognized one; it was to him the government would now have to go if it wanted to say something to the Protestant community in Egypt or ask something of it.

Later, the Rev. Safwat Naguib El Bayadi was elected vice-president, and Dr Imad Ramzi, a lay Evangelical leader, was appointed general secretary. Two more deputy presidents were later added, the Rev. Baqi Sadaqa Girgis for Assiut Province and the Rev. Fayez Faris for Minia Province.

As time went on, Sam's various activities propelled him to ever greater public prominence, and by the late Eighties he had become a well known public figure, invited to government and top church functions and regularly pictured in the secular press.

But he was not without his detractors. There were those who were jealous that he now wore two important hats; the first as president of the Protestant Churches of Egypt and secondly as founder and general director of CEOSS, the largest Christian development agency in Egypt and a vital force in the country's renewal, with its roots in the Evangelical Church. Sam was regularly being invited to all the major church events around the country. His presence was a visible sign of his expanded role in Egyptian religious and social life and spoke much about his role as a Protestant church leader.

His high profile, almost alone among Protestant leaders, and the independence and prestige CEOSS enjoyed, without reference to the Synod since its registration with the Ministry of Social Affairs, together stirred up jealousy and resentment among certain church leaders. In addition to this his desire to get things done, if necessary by occasionally circumventing the church bureaucracy, got him into hot water with some leading clergy.

Matters came to a head in 1992, when Sam came under personal attack in the Synod. He was totally devastated by the onslaught of allegations and charges directed against him, which mainly revolved around management issues, questions of control within the church community and the degree of authority Sam exercised in his various leadership roles. Some felt he was operating at a much too high a public level, with a private political agenda of his own. They suspected his motives, and would have preferred that he maintain a more low-key style.

Yet in the face of this personal onslaught, Samuel Habib fell silent and remained that way throughout the whole ordeal, refusing to answer his critics publicly because of the hurtful and untrue nature of their charges against him. What they said grieved and wounded him deeply. These were men he had known for a lifetime, and so their accusations were particularly painful to him.

Because of his continuing silence in public, a small group of pastors from the Synod came to Sam privately to discuss issues with him. His answers to their questions satisfied them. The Synod was duly informed; everyone was persuaded that Sam was speaking the truth; and so the matter was closed.

Relations between Sam and his detractors were somewhat improved by efforts to involve others more closely in the business of the church, and reconciliation was achieved. But Sam also had many colleagues who were supportive of him both in the Synod and outside of it. The CEOSS staff and board understood what he was facing and were prayerfully supportive of him. They understood the reasons behind the attack and felt Sam's pain keenly. But the effect of the whole process, and the accusations, took their toll on Sam's health. On June 1, 1992 he suffered a mild heart attack and was briefly hospitalized.

The shock had been too much. He had internalized all his emotions and hidden his true feelings throughout the ordeal, refusing to tell anyone of the real pain he was feeling. His collapse was sudden and shocked the community. He stayed in hospital for ten days, returning home on June 11.

Fawzia, his wife, who had stood by Sam throughout the entire ordeal, had felt Sam's pain and shared his suffering. Convinced that only jealousy lay behind the charges and nothing of any real substance, she rallied round her husband, giving him the strong support he needed.

Over the next few weeks she helped Sam reach the point where he could forgive his accusers. As he slowly recovered, Sam realized that the only thing he could do was to ask God to forgive and help him to forgive those who had falsely accused him, and said and done these things against him. He would try to forgive, even though he could never forget.

His faith, strengthened by years of service with numerous ups and downs, had taught him the powerful lesson of the need to forgive. Indeed it was his father who had taught him, by example, the lesson of letting go and moving on. It was a wise lesson indeed. If he worried all the time about what people thought, nothing would get done. He would be incapacitated and unable to function. Samuel Habib had been in the forefront of the battle far too long to let criticism kill him. But it had been a close call.

Changing church leaders' attitudes and forgiving jealousy was even harder, he discovered, than changing the poverty-ridden conditions in which so many of Egypt's people lived. Yet there were encouraging signs of hope over the years that different churches and denominations could in fact change their attitudes, or at least discuss their problems and differences.

It was through the Protestant Church Council, under Sam's leadership, that a dialogue with the Coptic Orthodox Church was first organized, at the request of His Holiness Pope Shenouda III. Over a three-year period, from 1988 to 1990, at Pope Shenouda's urging, the two groups studied two central but highly controversial doctrines: those of salvation and baptism.

While both sides agreed on the need for salvation and baptism, they could not find common ground theologically on either issue. The dialogue, however, did bring a deeper understanding between the two churches, and better relationships were established all round. The walls of hostility that had sometimes gone up between them over the decades now began to come down. The very fact that these dialogues were going on at all was an extraordinary milestone and provoked considerable commentary in the news-papers. Their resolutions and discussions, together with photos, were published in church magazines for the laity of both churches to see, as well as in the secular press. Public exposure was viewed positively by both sides.

On the subject of baptism they found that they could all agree on a number of issues including infant baptism, baptism as a sacrament, performing baptism in the name of the trinity, and that all Christians should observe it. Where they disagreed was on the Orthodox Church's insistence that the baptism of children was for the remission of sins.

In the Evangelical (Presbyterian) Church of Egypt, baptism of the new-born was meant to affirm the covenant God had with the child, and the parents' commitment to raise the child in the faith and prepare him or her for adult confirmation, when as a more mature person he or she would affirm publicly in faith what had been done for him at birth, and be received into the church.

The issue became thornier and more complex because the Coptic Orthodox Church did not recognize baptism in either the Catholic or Protestant Churches in Egypt. If an Orthodox person married a Catholic or Protestant he or she had to be rebaptized by immersion. The churches could not reach agreement on this issue, but at least they were talking. They agreed to disagree.

In the late 1980's a protocol agreement was reached among the

Protestant Churches of Egypt staking out areas of cooperation and principles of how they might work together. It was agreed that no pastor would leave one denomination for another unless for deep theological reasons that he could defend publicly. The protocol also set forth procedures for avoiding church splits, and stated that churches should refrain from stealing converts from one another.

In March 1993 an historic public meeting was held in Cairo, bringing together pastors and laity from all the Protestant Churches in Egypt, and a number of participants from other Middle Eastern Arab countries. The gathering, which was Sam's brainchild, included Anglicans, Presbyterians, Methodists, Plymouth (Exclusive) Brethren, Open Brethren, Baptists, Assemblies of God and numerous other smaller denominational groups. It included a time of public worship, concluding in an unprecedented communion service led by the heads of all the denominations.

At this historic occasion Samuel Habib told the more than 1,000 assembled leaders that even though Christians were a minority in Egypt, the churches had a responsibility and a mission to carry out. They must stand firmly together and complement each other's work. He argued forcefully, in a dynamic speech, that they must build strategies of co-operation in the hope that shared spiritual and social goals would bring about unity among them.

A number of Evangelical pastors from churches in other Arab nations, including Lebanon, Syria, Jordan, Sudan, Iraq and Bahrain, also shared in the leadership of the programme. The meeting lasted only a day, but it had a major impact on all those present. Protestant Christian unity was visible in a way that had never been seen before, and Samuel Habib believes it will have years of lasting effect on the Protestant Christian community in the Arab world.

For a brief moment the cracked and splintered face of Middle East Protestantism, so often torn by denominational factionalism, was patched up to show a unity the like of which had never been seen before. It was a victorious moment for Samuel Habib, man of peace and unity.

Samuel Habib views the present trend in Egypt towards greater vitality in church life both hopefully and positively. He sees the hand of God working out his mysterious will in people's lives, as extremism in Egyptian society and the sense of being a minority draw them closer together, and heighten their concern to attend church and to worship God. That Sam has had a hand in that is no small achievement. That he gives God all the glory demonstrates his modesty.

Within the General Evangelical Council of the Protestant Churches of Egypt, of which Samuel Habib is president, co-operative activities now take place in which the churches support one another despite the denominational and doctrinal differences that separate some of them.

As a result, churches like the Assemblies of God and the Church of Faith, a branch of Methodism, have doubled their membership in recent years.

The Anglican Church, too, is strong in its social outreach, as well as in its educational and medical work. It also owns a publishing house in Egypt – the Literature Board of the Episcopal (Anglican) Church.

Evangelical schools, established by American missionaries of the Presbyterian Church (U.S.A.) and given over to the Synod of the Nile in 1960, are among the finest educational institutions in the country. The Rev. Safwat Naguib El Bayadi, the present General Director of the Synod Schools Board, does a magnificent job of maintaining these schools and enabling them to keep up their good work. And a hospital in Tanta, in the heart of the Nile Delta, established by American missionaries and later given to the Synod of the Nile, is one of the most successful church-run hospitals in the country.

Samuel Habib is especially close to His Beatitude Patriarch Stephanos II, Patriarch of the Coptic Catholic Church, the largest of the Catholic Churches in Egypt. Over the years they have become particularly close friends.

The Coptic Catholic Church has always been very concerned about social work in Egypt. In recent years it has an increasingly ecumenical outlook, and its clergy work well with CEOSS staff in a variety of ways in many communities.

Caritas, an international Catholic lay organization involved in worldwide renewal, is also very active in Egypt, as is Catholic Relief Services. Catholic church schools, meanwhile, have the well-deserved reputation of being among the best in Egypt. They are among the elite of schools in the land and have maintained their heritage and standards at the highest possible levels. These schools are attended by both Muslims and Christians, and turn out some of the best graduates entering government service in the country. Many of today's highest political officials attended and graduated from these schools.

Chapter 8

A Theology of Hope

A BRIEF HISTORY

Christianity came to Egypt at the time of the first apostles. Mark, the author of the first gospel, is traditionally regarded as the founder of Egyptian Christianity following the events of Pentecost. Egyptian Jews who were converted to Christianity after listening to Peter's preaching recorded in Acts 2, returned to Egypt and preached the gospel there. By the 5th century Egypt was totally Christian.

The theological war fought over the two natures of Christ at the Council of Chalcedon in 394 AD did not help matters between Christians. After vigorous debate, the Coptic Orthodox Church supported the one nature of Jesus Christ while all the other branches of Christendom, including the Eastern Orthodox churches (Copts, Syrians and Armenians) and the Roman Catholic church, pronounced their support for the two natures of Jesus Christ.

The monastic system established by the Greek Orthodox and Catholic churches was essentially isolationist in character, and while it spread around the world its roots were in Egyptian soil and had its primary impetus in the Coptic Orthodox Church.

The church maintained its dominance in Egypt till the 7th century, when Islam entered the country and many Christians converted to the new religion. By the end of the century more than thirty percent of the population was Muslim. A further wave of conversions in the 10th century brought most of the rest of the country into Islam. Today Muslims outnumber Christians in Egypt by a ratio of ten to one.

European interest in Egypt saw intervention first by the French in the early 19th century and then by the British from the late 19th century up to the middle of the 20th century. The meeting of Eastern and Western cultures during more than a century of colonialism led to efforts to modernize Islam, and an enlightened desire to combine traditional religious thought with the best of modern rationalism and scientific progress. In 1926 the Muslim Brotherhood was set up largely in opposition to secularist and nationalist trends.

After World War II, Egypt became increasingly committed to the Arab cause in Palestine, and its unexpected defeat in the first of a series of Arab-Israeli wars contributed to disillusionment and political unrest. The creation of a new political establishment in Egypt between 1952 and 1956 sealed the end of colonialism. A new political order had been inaugurated in the Middle East.

Since 1977 Egypt has been governed by the National Democratic Party under an elected president, first Anwar Sadat and then Hosni Mubarak.

In recent years the government has been struggling to contain waves of Islamic fundamentalism in the country's slums and rural backwaters, as well as acute economic difficulties and a booming population.

The 19th century saw the Coptic Orthodox Church at its lowest ebb. It was institutionally weak and ineffectual. The monasteries could not produce enough educated monks to turn the situation around. Islam was now the religion of the majority of people.

A number of Catholic priests had come to Egypt and established the Roman Catholic Church; and in 1822 the first Anglican mission came to Egypt. Prior to that a number of other Protestant missions, like the Moravians, had tried and failed to establish a foothold, but the Anglicans arrived and stayed. They attracted few members but established schools and hospitals and set up the first Christian publishing house in Egypt.

Thirty-two years later, in 1854, a Scottish Presbyterian missionary, John Hogg, arrived in Egypt to preach the gospel. His purpose was not to establish a new church but simply to preach the gospel. Later that year, missionaries arrived in Egypt from the United Presbyterian Church of North America and established the indigenous Evangelical Church in Egypt.

The Presbyterian Church had no intention of forming or founding a new mission. Its purpose was to reform the Coptic Orthodox Church from within and work with it, not against it.

However, the Patriarch of the Coptic Orthodox Church excommunicated the new mission, and as a result a new church was established in 1899 under the name 'Synod of the Nile of the Evangelical Church of Egypt'.

The missionaries were members of the Synod, but from the outset it was made clear that the church was national and its pastoral work would be totally supported by Egyptian funds, with missionary funds maintaining only general services. The church's goal, from the very beginning, was to ensure that pastors received all their support locally, with the church being very much a national church run by the Synod of the Nile.

In 1854 the Presbyterian Church introduced the Arabic Bible into Egypt. It had been translated in Lebanon and was now freely distributed among Egyptian Christians. In 1926 an Evangelical Theological Seminary was established in Cairo to meet the growing demands of the new churches springing up throughout the country. The building was constructed by Egyptians with funds drawn from the national church in Egypt.

A new era in Egyptian Protestant Christianity now began in earnest. From the very beginning, missions working with the churches established schools and founded hospitals all over the country. At first they were run by foreign missionaries, but later nationals assumed leadership of all the institutions they established.

The primary concern of the church was that the gospel of Jesus Christ should be freely presented to men and women, and that it should revolve around faith and action rather than faith and ritual.

This was an important and fundamental difference between the ancient, creedal Coptic Orthodox Church and the new, independent Protestant missionary churches. The faith presented by Evangelicals was a faith not only of the heart but of everyday life as well. The result of all this was that a number of leaders in the Coptic Orthodox Church, monks and members of Egypt's intelligentsia, as well as both rich and poor people, caught this new vision and joined the Evangelical Church.

A PRACTICAL THEOLOGY

Samuel Habib grew up being taught that the main task of the church leader was to preach the gospel, and that the main focus of the theologically trained was to become a pastor. But what he saw as he travelled around Egypt was the appalling conditions most of his people lived in. To focus solely on being a church pastor meant confining the gospel to just a few well-educated people who could read, write and understand the Good News. Illiteracy isolated millions from ever reading the Word of God for themselves.

For the church not to see the value of literature and literacy work was to blindfold itself to the needs of millions of people. Samuel Habib simply could not blind himself to the enormous needs of millions of his people. He felt called to change that. His heart ached for Egypt's millions. In his mind serving illiterates and the poor was not an option but a requisite of the gospel, and just as important as ministering to a few well- educated people. To reach out to the impoverished and poor in spirit was to reach out like Jesus did, and to serve them in exactly the same way as his Lord and Master. This was the motivating force behind Sam's desire to devote his early years to literacy work. He turned his focus then to serving the poor in general, and illiterates in particular, as his primary role, while continuing to preach in churches across Egypt.

The early years were difficult and an uphill struggle as he sought to focus and refocus the church's efforts. His labours were not always appreciated by his friends or by the broader Christian community. There was little sympathy and even less understanding for what he was trying to do. It was only in the late 1950s that some of Egypt's top Christian leaders began to see the importance of what he was doing and the vital part he was playing in the church's outreach and in reshaping the church's vision.

But Samuel Habib was plumbing the Bible's depths, focusing particularly on the gospels. The more he read, the clearer his understanding of Jesus's mission became to him. Again he read the same stories, but this time with different eyes. He saw in the parable of the ten lepers a model for his own mission. Jesus, without hesitation, cured the ten but only one came back to thank him; nine did not. From this Samuel Habib concluded that the nine were never presented with the gospel, but that their bodies and the humiliating, disowning disease they carried with them were nevertheless important to Jesus. By curing them, Jesus made clear the importance he placed on them simply as human beings made in the image of God. They were of value to his heavenly Father and therefore to himself, and he loved them with the compassion of the Father regardless of whether or not they accepted him as Lord and Saviour or as Israel's hope in the expected Messiah.

But the one leper who did return to thank Jesus was given another opportunity to know who he was and to believe on him in a deeper way. And it was only after he believed in Jesus for salvation that he received forgiveness for his sins.

From this Samuel Habib drew the following conclusions. Jesus had two missions. The first was his calling to evangelize, to announce the Good News, to proclaim the liberating message of the gospel, to bring people out of darkness into light. This was Jesus's primary task: to persuade people, without coercion or manipulation, to come to know him and accept him as Lord and Saviour. Jesus's second mission was to help people become more fully human: human beings as God created them from the very beginning. He wanted them to be whole and live life fully.

In his healing ministry, Jesus sought to cure people of their diseases because he saw behind those diseases the consequences of the Fall. His desire was that people should have life abundant, and live out God's plan as he intended it for them in the world he had created.

From his reading and understanding of Scripture, Samuel Habib concluded that it was profoundly against God's will that people should live in poverty or protracted pain and suffering. This was not God's desire for mankind. A loving father's desire for his children is that they should live in peace and security, not in poverty and shame.

From his reading of history, Sam saw how, in communities and nations, people lorded it over one another and made distinctions between master and slave, male and female, elevating the rich above the poor, the dominant over the submissive, the powerful over the powerless. But the Christian faith, if rightly understood, levels the playing field for everybody. Jesus humbled himself, 'taking the form of a bond-servant', identifying himself totally with humans in their need.

Sam's understanding of the apostle Paul's teaching was that 'in Christ' no class or gender distinctions were permitted or tolerated. Those who had accepted Jesus as Lord and Saviour are united to him as one people without distinction of gender, race or colour, poverty or wealth, and therefore every effort had to be made to break down the barriers that exist between people. Sam saw in the biblical doctrine of creation the divine hand of a loving God creating man in his own image. God creates both male and female, endowing them with gifts and making them equal; and in the freedom he bestows upon them, they can choose to worship him. Because of sin, man is set psychologically against himself, sociologically against his neighbour, and theologically against God. Social injustice curses mankind. Feudal lords and masters become the oppressors, and servants and slaves the oppressed. Wars erupt between peoples, women became enslaved to men, poverty abounds and injustices intensify. The clenched fist becomes the symbol of might and power holding sway over people's lives, rather than the open hand of love and compassion.

Samuel Habib sees the role of Christians in imitating their Lord's example of ministry, bringing the word of redemption and healing to whomever they meet, wherever they travel, and in assisting human communities to regain their history and dignity, as the Biblical narrative in Genesis chapters 1 and 2 makes clear. The Creation, as God intended it before sin entered into the world, as recorded in Genesis chapter 3, is the ideal. From Sam's perspective this is the way Jesus wants God's will in creation to be implemented.

Men and women would be equal, as would masters and slaves, rich and poor. The dignity of all human beings would be respected, asserted and supported. Men and women might differ in the gifts God gave them, but the infinite worth of every human being was absolute and inviolable.

Sam Habib contends that as we look at the New Testament we can see situations where Jesus healed people without ever preaching to them about his messiahship and lordship. It is also apparent that there were situations in which Jesus only preached to people about his messiahship without ever healing them, and then there were situations in which Jesus both healed and preached to people at the same time.

From these instances Sam concludes that it is possible to view Jesus's healing ministry as an end in itself, while his ministry of reconciliation, that is, of bringing people to a saving faith, was a separate goal. Both goals, Sam maintains, are the responsibility of the church. They coexist along two parallel lines, each complementing the other.

Jesus respected the dignity of all human beings. He coerced no one. He violated no person's free will. He always invited people to come to him and accept his kingship. He accepted their rejection of him with profound sorrow and pain if that was their choice.

Sam saw in the gospels that many people were healed by Jesus during his lifetime and ministry but were never saved. Many who heard the Good News of the gospel accepted Christ's invitation; others heard the gospel but did not respond. Jesus nevertheless healed them because he loved them and because they were made in the image of God.

The Doctrine of Creation and the Doctrine of the Atonement are the two most basic doctrines in the Bible. They complement each other and cannot be separated from each other. Over the course of time, the church of Jesus Christ became so involved with the Doctrine of the Atonement that it neglected the Doctrine of Creation. Yet, Sam maintains, the Doctrine of Creation reveals God to us as the Father of all humanity, of all people everywhere. The whole world is his world.

If Jesus were here today in Egypt, Sam Habib contends, he would serve both Muslim and Christian alike. He would not show favouritism or separate out and classify people. One has only to look at how he treated the Samaritan woman and a Jewish man. Jesus was no respecter of persons. The two were clearly different in race and doctrine, but Jesus did not favour the Jew over the Samaritan or vice versa. He viewed them both as sons and daughters of creation.

Sam maintains that the church misunderstands Jesus's calling because it fails to see his dual role. As Christians it is imperative that we see the humanity and creatureliness of man as intrinsic in itself, while also seeing man's need for salvation through Christ as a separate but equal response and necessity. We are all children of God by creation, but those who accept Christ as Lord and Saviour are sons and daughters by redemption.

In his love of people Jesus showed no partiality. Sam sees this borne out particularly in Jesus's support for women. What he did for the Samaritan woman broke all Jewish custom and stepped over the line created by Jewish tradition. In fact he was despised for his actions by the Jewish community. Jesus's respect for the woman caught in adultery, and later for Mary Magdalene, illustrated his support and advocacy for womanhood in a manner unprecedented for his time. Jesus demonstrated that he not only cared for women but also confirmed and established their inherent equality with men.

Sam sees, in the story of the woman caught in adultery, Jesus's total compassion for her as a person and for all those caught up in men's abuse, while Jewish religious leaders simply wanted to stone her to death. Jesus's refusal to condemn her also contradicted their absolute standards of right and wrong.

In short, Jesus presents us with a whole new view of womanhood that went against all the cultural and religious norms of his day and still has the power to shock and embarrass the contemporary church. In Sam's mind the church has no option but to follow its master, even if it means going against prevailing cultural standards. Only fear and tradition stand in the way.

In Jesus's refusal to condemn the adulteress, and his decision ultimately to forgive her, he wanted to make it clear that the man involved was also complicit in the act of adultery, not just the woman. Both were equally guilty before God; both needed to repent, and so did the self-righteous Jewish community that sought to stone her.

Sam sees in Jesus's support for women, children and the down-trodden a model for the church to follow. Jesus respected the inherent dignity of all people. There were no exceptions with him. In the story of blind Bartimaeus, Sam sees the issue of his dignity and faith as inherently more important to Jesus than the healing and restoring of his sight. That was of secondary importance. Spiritual blindness was infinitely worse in Jesus's eyes than physical blindness.

This was equally true in the case of Jesus's support for low-caste people, the poor, women and children. Jesus went out of his way to speak to women and be embraced by them, accepted their ministrations to him, and recognized their inherent worth against a hostile Jewish culture and an equally hostile secular, Roman, culture. The church's task therefore, is to emulate Jesus's concern for women as if it were Jesus himself.

Sam observes that what Jesus did also had political overtones and ramifications for the community at large. He cites Jesus's entrance into Jerusalem as one particular illustration. The people wanted a big parade, the triumphal entry of a victorious Messiah on a white horse. Jesus chose a donkey, the humblest of animals, on which to enter Jerusalem.

He entered during Pentecost as a leader of the community. The people shouted to him, recognizing his leadership and authority, but Jesus chose not to be a leader in the sense they wanted. He saw leadership in terms of servanthood, a way to change society that puts God first, not naked power; a society that believes and trusts in God, a society that takes its ethical and moral values from the Bible to guide and lead it.

In Jesus, Sam sees no dichotomy between public and private faith. The leaders of the Jewish community were also the leaders in the synagogue; the roles of the two were intertwined. The external trappings of religion had to correspond to genuine heartfelt obedience. Anything less was hypocrisy.

Sam interprets Jesus's attempt to purify the Temple as an attack on the top-ranking business leadership of the day. These were the property-owners, the money-lenders, the powerful and the rich who had sanction for what they did from the religious leaders. Jesus attacked the merchandise-owners in the Temple and threw them out because they dared to desecrate God's house and turn it from a place of worship into a commercial zone. His attack was symbolically an attack against the religious leaders of the people and against those who ran the Temple, turning it away from its true purpose as a place to worship God and to pray.

Jesus also wanted a changed social order, a society built on the ethics of faith rather than on sin and greed. Samuel Habib contends that when we look at what Jesus' ministry was all about, we see him wanting to transform the individual and the community, yearning for people to take a long hard look at their lives and to take issues of justice and morality seriously.

Christians are called upon specifically to do justice, to practise righteousness, to be honest, to be loyal and faithful in their dealings with each other people, and to uphold the general good of the community rather than seek personal gain, ambition, power or status.

When we look at people, Sam argues, we cannot separate body from soul, the spiritual from the social or the economic realities of people's lives. All are one. 'If I am honest, I am honest when I pray and honest in my commerce. I am honest in my relationships with my friends. We must see human beings in their wholeness. We must not categorize people into different parts and separate those parts out. The spiritual, social and material are one and must be viewed as one. All human beings have a common humanity and unity, and if we are going to take care of people we must treat the whole person, not just his spiritual life and forget that he is flesh and blood.'

A hungry man, says Sam, will never hear the liberating message of salvation in Christ if he is swamped by poverty and hunger. The church must take care of his human wants before it can minister seriously to his spiritual needs.

The church, from its Spirit-filled beginnings at Pentecost, has shown concern for the poor. It has given money and food for the hungry on certain and specific occasions. Helping people in this way is good, but it is not enough, says Sam. Relief is only part of the picture. A person can become dependent on those who help him. In the long run this is not good. One major problem with aid is that it puts one person over another. It puts the receiver in the position of the supplicant, and does not recognize the intrinsic equality of all human beings.

Sam argues that those privileged Christians who have been given much must work alongside the poor. The church needs to be involved in development. In development we help the person find a craft that gives him regular work. To give a poor man a loan to use his skills and let him repay it over a period of time legitimates his inherent worth. In this way his dignity is maintained and he stands on an equal footing with the giver. 'That person is not dependent on me, nor totally independent of me. We become interdependent on each other. He is a respected person in his or her own right and should be treated as such.' Sam believes it is time the church examined and brought together theological and Biblical issues with social justice and development concerns, so that individuals, groups and communities can become more human in finding their resources for development with their own thinking. It is only then that the lives of people will radically improve.

This has been one of the most neglected areas down through the years in the church's life, and it must be reclaimed, contends Sam. It means study and technical assistance. It is a task the church must take seriously and be responsible for, while it continues to preach the gospel of Jesus Christ to lost sinners.

Chapter 9

Christian and Muslim: Can They Live Together?

On November 13, 1992 the Mufti of Egypt, Dr. Sheikh Mohammed Sayed Tantawi, the second-highest ranking Muslim religious
cleric in Egypt, solemnly entered the Evangelical Church in
Heliopolis, Cairo accompanied by Dr. Samuel Habib.

It was an historic moment in the religious life of Egypt. The
Mufti had come to address a meeting on 'Religion and the
Advancement of the Community', and his appearance demonstrated remarkable courage in the face of growing militancy among
an increasing number of Muslim fundamentalists. It also sent a loud
signal to both Muslims and the Christian community that no
amount of violence by these militant fanatics would sever the deep
relationships forged over the years between the two religions.
Despite historic ups and downs between Christians and Muslims, a
new respect for each other's positions had emerged due to the efforts
of many sincere people like Samuel Habib. There was now a
growing understanding between the two powerful religious bodies
that had not previously existed.

For more than a year Sam Habib, together with a group of other
leaders, had worked quietly but persistently behind the scenes to
make such an occasion possible. It was a tremendous diplomatic
triumph for Egypt's Protestant leader, and one loaded with sym-
bolism. It was also a personal achievement for the Rev. Makram
Naguib, pastor of the Heliopolis church, who in his broad-minded
concern for national unity and peace had supportively shared in
planning the Mufti's reception in his church.

Both Muslims and Christians had been invited to attend, and
both groups appeared in large numbers. The church that evening
was packed. The Mufti was received cordially by the mixed
audience. It was not an occasion for proselytism by Muslims or
evangelism by Christians, but simply an opportunity for followers

of both religions to find ways to communicate with each other, seek common ground wherever possible, and move forward together.

The occasion received tremendous public attention in Egypt and was thoroughly reported in the newspapers and on television. Sam Habib, who had extended the invitation to the Mufti, spoke on behalf of Egypt's Protestant community. He talked about Egypt's pressing need for social development, which was of common concern to both Christians and Muslims and a possible area for fruitful co-operation. Dr. Mohammed Salim El Awwa, a lawyer, Cairo University professor and prominent Muslim thinker, also spoke on the theme announced for the occasion, and the gathering also brought together many other distinguished people from the wider community.

Christians had invited Muslims to attend the gathering, thus affording an opportunity to build new relationships. Walls of suspicion which had been building for years began to break down. While not all Christians and Muslims approved of the meeting and many boycotted it, it was, from Sam Habib's point of view, and by general agreement, an overwhelming success in Christian-Muslim communication. While no miracles occurred, it was nevertheless a significant breakthrough and an example of what could be done by both groups reaching out to each other. The occasion promoted much dialogue and clearly advanced a better mutual understanding. Above all, it sought to ease the tensions between Muslims and Christians in Egypt.

In his speech, the Mufti underscored the on-going good relationships between Christians and Muslims and denounced what he called the criminal acts of extremists, contending that they did not speak for Islam. He repeatedly told his audience that Islam was a religion of peace and would remain tolerant of Christians and Christianity. This was sweet music to Christian ears. He reiterated that historically Christians and Muslims had lived in peace alongside each other for centuries in Egypt, and that regardless of the current wave of fanaticism and the violent behaviour of a few fundamentalists, the Christian minority would continue to be treated equally and given their rights.

In the turbulent world of the Middle East no greater passions are stirred than those of competing religious beliefs, as Sam Habib knows well. For half a century he has walked a fragile tightrope, practising his Christian convictions in a largely Muslim world. In the words of Jesus, he has had to be as wise as a serpent and harmless as a dove.

In a country of 59 million people, a quarter of the Arab world's population, followers of the non-militant Muslim Brotherhood are thought to number half a million or more. Membership of other fundamentalist groups is estimated at some 200,000, though no more than 10,000 are believed to be hard-core militants prepared to use violence in pursuit of their goal of creating a pure Islamic state. Christians, mostly Coptic Orthodox, account for only ten percent of Egypt's population.

It is not uncommon in some privately-owned mosques in Cairo today to hear white-robed Islamic militants, gathering in defiance of a government ban, call for revolution. Speaker after speaker urges followers to struggle against non-believers: secularists, communists, Christians, Jews and the 'infidels who rule Egypt'. All these different groups are seen by Muslim extremists as fiercely opposed to Islam. It is not a message the majority of Muslims, and certainly Egypt's Christians, want to hear, and the government has tried to stop this sort of inflammatory preaching.

Into this political and religious turmoil, Sam Habib and those who labour with him in the ministry of CEOSS daily walk with faith, boldness and hope, living proof that to follow Jesus means taking up one's cross daily and following him.

The truth is, Sam Habib sees what the militants see: the grinding poverty that oppresses so many, in stark contrast to the privileged lifestyle of the elite. He watches as the militants provide funds for the destitute, open shelters, run clinics, mediate disputes and patrol the streets against common crime, while continuously railing against government graft and corruption and, in the case of a small minority, committing acts of terrorism. But for the gentle yet persistent Sam Habib, the solutions lie not in violence and government overthrow but in the non-violent and peaceful way of Jesus.

History has not been altogether kind to Christians in the Middle East where Christianity has been fighting an uphill struggle to survive for centuries. In fact it might even thrive better as a minority culture, certainly becoming purer in faith and doctrine. No one ever said the way would be easy, or promised a pot of gold at the end of the proverbial rainbow.

If Christians are going to survive in Egypt, Sam maintains, they must seriously consider establishing solid working relationships with the larger Muslim community, and take the initiative in building closer ties and better understanding between the groups.

On the one hand, Christians need to understand Islam as a modern Muslim presents it. This doesn't mean that Christians have to suddenly agree with Muslim beliefs. But at the very least Christians should understand the basic tenets of Islam without feeling threatened. For their part, Muslims should understand Christianity as a modern Arab Christian believes it. Sam Habib believes that a mutual understanding of each other's beliefs would increase the respect of each group for the other. Respect is not the same as acquiescing in the other person's beliefs, but it does value the other's point of view, build better understanding and improve relationships. Caricatures and stereotypes of each other's religion only hurt, and drive unnecessary wedges between people.

There are many areas, Sam Habib maintains, in which Muslims and Christians can work together. In the sphere of social concern where the overriding needs of the people are obvious, Christians and Muslims can and should unite and work together. In this way it is possible to build communities where Christians and Muslims can coexist in peace.

Sam Habib would like to see Christians and Muslims establish a joint society for social outreach, to work together on one project serving both the community and the country. Working together, Sam Habib has learned, breaks down barriers, creates better understanding, and develops the nation as a whole.

The Protestant leader sees a powerful Biblical image to support his claim in the history of the Israelites forced into captivity by Nebuchadnezzar, King of Babylon, found in the 39th and 40th chapters of Jeremiah. In Sam Habib's understanding of the Babylonian Captivity, Nebuchadnezzar took hostages from Jerusalem into Babylon where the people of God were asked to share in the life of the community: 'Do not be afraid to serve the Babylonians. Settle down in the land and serve the king of Babylon, and it will go well with you.'

But many of them refused. The Israelites, in exile, did not want to be a part of the Babylonian culture. They also did not want to be involved in the broader Babylonian community. Because they were sad, they would not even sing the songs of Zion in the face of their Babylonian oppressors.

Jeremiah told them to build homes and live, cultivate gardens and eat the fruits of the land, marry and bring forth sons and daughters. With the people of God the problem was that they continually disobeyed God and kept the faith of their fathers to themselves. They would not share the knowledge of Jehovah with their captors.

Sam Habib draws from this the lesson that Christians in Egypt must be positive and live in the community they have been privileged to be born into and not isolate themselves from those around them. To suffer alienation is an act of the will which must be resisted at all costs. It only creates fear and loathing. In communities across Egypt, and throughout all Arab countries, the feelings of togetherness can be strengthened so that one can say: 'This is my land, to serve and to work for.' If God has destined Christians to live in Egypt as part of the nation, however numerically small their community might be, then it is incumbent upon them to play an integral part in serving the people as God would have them serve, and not to be like foreigners and strangers. In this way, Sam Habib argues, Christians can both feel safe living in the community and contribute to its ongoing health.

Even though problems exist, and they always will, people should not exaggerate them, and Christians should not let themselves suffer persecution complexes. To be psychologically and spiritually healthy God intends Christians to be active in society as both lay people and clergy to serve that community.

One problem Sam Habib sees in being a minority group in the overwhelming majority situation in Egypt is the feeling of isolation and alienation. This only breeds an unhealthy fear in Christians and makes them want to withdraw and must be resisted at all costs. Christians can and should integrate into their communities, while not losing their identity. Christians are called to be salt and light to the world, and so to love their Muslim neighbours as Christ would. Integration does not mean absorption. Egyptian Christians should be a living expression, witness and testimony to the love of God in Christ to the wider community.

The way of love is not impossible, however strewn with hate the path might seem. Sam Habib has shown that real, unselfish love is possible. He has gone before, holding high the torch of truth for all to see. It is now up to all his fellow-Christians to look up, see the flame and follow it bravely.

Chapter 10

Prophecy and the Prophet

WHO SPEAKS FOR GOD?

Raba' Ibrahim El Shrafi, a 53-year-old mother of seven and resident of a rundown refugee camp in the Gaza Strip, quietly went about her business shopping at the local market. Without warning, Israeli security forces moved in, tossing tear gas into the crowded marketplace. Seconds later Raba' began to choke. Within minutes she was dead. The poisonous gas had done its deadly work.

Between December 1987 and March 1994 some 1,365 Palestinian men, women and children were killed as a direct result of Israeli Defence forces, border guards, collaborators and settlers in the state of Israel. Hundreds more have been beaten, had their homes sealed or destroyed and their lives and livelihoods threatened by the occupying troops. Human rights monitors reported that 1993 was the worst-ever year for human rights conditions and violations in the Israeli-occupied territories of the Gaza Strip, the Golan Heights and the West Bank.

A number of Israeli soldiers too have been killed by members of Hamas, an extremist Palestinian organization, who have also killed and wounded Jewish settlers. It is a vicious tit-for-tat game with no winners, just an endless cycle of killing and death. Among Palestinians can be found both Muslims and Christians.

During the years of struggle many have found themselves thrown out of their homes and onto the streets by the Israelis.

Samuel Habib has numerous Palestinian friends, among them some who, with tears in their eyes recall the events that cost them their homes, jobs and families.

Samuel Habib is not quick to judge, however. In a world of extremes and opposites he knows and counts himself among those who are not against the Jewish people themselves, but often at odds with their political leadership.

He understands only too well what it means to be both a struggling minority and a survivor in his own country, one that has experienced colonialism and oppression. Yet he is disturbed that the Jews, who for thousands of years knew little but persecution, are themselves playing the role of persecutors when it comes to their Arab neighbours.

From where he sits in Cairo the chequered political landscape of the Middle East deeply troubles the Christian soul of Samuel Habib. Jews and Arabs have been pitted against each other for decades, with only increasing cycles of violence and bloodshed to show for it.

Egypt fought three disastrous wars with Israel on behalf of the Palestinians, and the accords signed at Camp David in 1978 by Prime Minister Menachem Begin and President Anwar Sadat, followed by their peace treaty the following year, heralded a diplomatic breakthrough. If Egypt could make peace with Israel, then so too could other Arab nations.

Now the Palestinians are making peace with Israel, and Jordan too has signed on in the peace initiatives, while other Arab nations are involved in gruelling negotiations.

The recent Israeli-Palestinian peace accord holds out hope and promise for a real and lasting peace in the Middle East. The future now looks better than it ever has done in this troubled corner of the world since Israel was established as a sovereign state, in 1948. Two leaders; Yasser Arafat, chairman of the Palestine Liberation Organization, and Yitzhak Rabin, the Israeli Prime Minister shook hands in the spirit of peace while the world looked on at this first breakthrough in 45 years, and pledged to work together towards a peaceful solution of their differences.

For Sam Habib it is the beginning of a whole new chapter in Middle East affairs, the sons of Ishmael and the sons of Isaac finally sitting down to break bread at the table of peace. Peace, of course, does not mean unity or even total harmony, but it is a hopeful beginning and infinitely better than the strife that has made this sliver of land a battleground for half a century. A real and lasting peace is now possible, held together for the moment with promises and handshakes.

Extremist groups on both sides seem to have little intention of accepting peace and have already denounced the peace accords, promising death to all those they see as betraying their cause. They know they still have an unsettling ability to upset the tenuous peace and push the two groups into war, or at least into terrorist blood-letting. It is a balancing act and anything is still possible.

But something that has also made Sam Habib unhappy in recent years is the near-hysterical support for Israel and its militaristic policies against the Palestinians and the Arab world in general, by millions of American fundamentalists and evangelicals who un-thinkingly endorse all that Israel does in the name of 'Biblical prophecy'.

For Sam the state of Israel is a reality. That Israel exists, and should be accepted as a legitimate nation state, is no longer in question. Israel should be permitted to live and coexist among its Arab neighbours.

When the 1917 Balfour Declaration pledged the British government to the 'establishment in Palestine of a national home for the Jewish people' it also stated with equal clarity 'that nothing shall be done which may prejudice the civil and religious rights of existing non-Jewish communities in Palestine'. Such has not always been the case in practice.

Yet Israel has been given unqualified support militarily and financially by the United States, even when it has clearly violated normal standards of civility and human behaviour. The powerful American Jewish lobby and the right-wing Christian lobby are two of the most powerful forces arrayed against the Arab world. While the Jewish lobby is understandable, the Christian lobby is troubling and wounding to Samuel Habib. What possible justification can there be for regarding a piece of real estate as having more intrinsic value than one human soul for whom Christ died?

Millions of Arab Christians are deeply offended by this unquali-fied support of Israel because of a hermeneutic that views the Bible through the narrow lens of Dispensationalism and sees God acting only on behalf of Israel, while ignoring millions of Arab Christians and Muslims.

Coupled with this are the stereotypical portraits of Arabs as furtive, violent and crazy, which serve only to enhance the image Westerners, particularly Americans, have of Arabs. And this is wrong. Sam Habib views this as a gross and inaccurate portrayal of Arabs and the Arab world. Certainly Western films and the media have not helped. The film 'Lawrence of Arabia' portrayed Arabs as little more than uncivilized nomads wandering the deserts killing everything in sight.

This sort of stereotyping troubles the gentle Christian soul of a man who has never lifted his hand to anyone, and who would rather run in the opposite direction than shoot a man or woman made in God's image, regardless of whether they are Jew or Arab.

The world stands divided over how to resolve political and religious differences in the Middle East, and the lop-sided view of Arabs so commonly portrayed in the West is deeply unhelpful.

Equally troubling to this gentle prophet are the views of millions of Christians in the West, mainly in the U.S., who allow Israel to do anything it wants to its Arab neighbours, especially the Palestinians in the occupied territories, because of the interpretation of certain Old Testament passages.

Dr. Habib is disturbed by such interpretations of Scripture, and argues that the Bible's message of reconciliation, peace and justice is being distorted and compromised when it sanctions policies of militarism and oppression by one group of people against another.

That Israel exists and should be allowed to live in peace with its Arab neighbours is now a fact of Middle East political life. The notion, endorsed by many American evangelicals and fundamentalists, that Israel has a divine right to the land, that is, all territory west of the River Jordan, based on the interpretation of certain texts in the Old Testament, is not so certain.

The dubious exegesis of these texts in the context of 20th century events, with no thought for a large proportion of the land's inhabitants, mostly Arabs, angers and troubles Sam Habib. To him it is clear that in the Old Testament God chose Israel to be a special people in covenant relationship with himself for a distinctive purpose: that through Israel all the nations of the earth would be blessed.

But it was an act of God's grace that he chose Israel, not a matter of Israel deserving it. God could have chosen stones from which to make sons of Abraham. He chose the people of Israel out of his love for them, which had no basis in Israel's goodness but in his own loving nature and character.

His choice of Israel, moreover, did not mean that God ceased to be sovereign over all the other peoples of the earth, including the Arab nations. God still retains his sovereign love as creator of the universe. He is still Father to the whole world and to all the peoples of the earth.

God chose Israel for a special purpose and mission. Israel was the first nation to know God by his name – Jehovah, the Lord, the One God; and it would be through Israel that all the peoples of the earth would come to know the one true God. Their main mission and task was to declare the Lord God of Israel to all the people of the earth.

Sam Habib believes that millions of Christians in the West misinterpret Genesis 12:3 to mean that God demands total and blind allegiance to Israel regardless of what it does to its Arab neighbours, and that to bless Israel is to invoke God's blessing while to oppose Israel is to invoke his wrath. This argument, sometimes known as the Abraham Factor, is upheld and dogmatically asserted by the Rev. Jerry Falwell and millions of fundamentalists like him.

No one single verse has been more widely used (and misused) than this one. As it is popularly construed in these circles, the verse establishes an eternal principle operating throughout human history, whereby nations that side with the Jewish people prosper while those that persecute the Jews come to ruin.

To give just one example of the absurdity of this position, and just how far some Christians are willing to carry this idea, a 'Genesis 12:3 Committee' lobby group in Washington DC was once organized to oppose selling weapons to Saudi Arabia on these spurious Scriptural grounds.

Proponents of the arms sale were threatened with divine retribution. In his book *Listen, America!* Falwell comments: 'I firmly believe God has blessed America because America has blessed the Jew.'

Even the most cursory reading of this verse shows the absurdity of such an application. The notion that a country would be doomed forever for not rendering 'allegiance to Israel' is a preposterous proposition nowhere even intimated in the Bible.

We have to see the Scriptures in their context, says Habib. Modern Israel is a secular state, not a religious one. Not all Jewish people are Zionists, and not all Jews support the present policies of the Israeli government, so Habib does not see any basis for giving preference to any particular national entity. Why, therefore, should American Christians give unqualified support to all that Israel does, especially to the Palestinians in the occupied territories?

If we look at the land question in the Old Testament it is clear that Jehovah demanded not only single-minded devotion to himself but also that the people practise social justice on the land if they wanted his continued blessing.

It is interesting to note that the only piece of land Abraham ever owned was purchased by him (Genesis 23). Moreover, merely possessing the promise does not justify the use of any means to acquire the land. The example of Abraham is noteworthy. Even though he had been guaranteed a vast stretch of land, there is no evidence that he ever tried to seize any of it by force.

Abraham was also willing to surrender the most fertile land in exchange for peace (Genesis 13). His son Isaac likewise withdrew from grazing lands to avoid strife with the original inhabitants (Gen.26:12–33).

Sam Habib argues that when the Israelites were disobedient towards Jehovah and in certain situations tried to reserve God for themselves, for their own benefit, they were scattered and suffered the humiliation of the Exile.

Sam Habib sees in the coming of Jesus Christ the last declaration of God to the world. The parable of the vineyard, Sam points out, is a parable of God's relationship with the world. The owner sends several messengers, all of whom are killed, until he finally sends his son who is God's last messenger and final revelation to the world.

Therefore any understanding of biblical events with regard to Israel and the Arab nations must be seen and interpreted in the light of Jesus Christ. The promise given by God to Abraham and his tribe, says Sam Habib, was fulfilled in Jesus Christ. It is in Jesus Christ that all God's promises are fulfilled (2 Cor.1:20); the old covenant is made redundant and should be excluded from consideration, apart from the implications of his coming. In his epistle to the Galatians (chapter 3), the apostle Paul argues that the true seed of Abraham to whom the covenant refers is Jesus Christ and all those, Jew and Gentile who confess his name, worship and bow down before him and own him as Lord.

It is important to remember that it is because we belong to Jesus Christ, and only when we are in proper relationship with him, that we fulfil the covenant.

We are not entitled to any special privileges because of our ancestry. And it is through Jesus that the Kingdom of God is fully realized and God's mission to the world is manifested, not only to Jews but to Gentiles as well.

Jesus came first to the House of Israel, but not exclusively to address the Jews. His mission broadened to include all the peoples of the earth. The Scripture is ratified in the declaration 'God so loved the world that He gave His son . . .' Implicit in this statement is the universality of God's concern for the whole world under the lordship of Jesus Christ. Therefore Jews are only the descendants of the sons of Abraham by blood line and birth. In the New Testament, true believers in Jesus Christ are the spiritual descendants of Abraham, called by God from every nation on earth, and are sons and daughters by reason of the New Birth.

The true Israel, then, is the people of God drawn from every nation of the world, including Israel and those Jews who acknowledge Jesus as Lord and are prepared to accept that mission, first given to the Israelites and then to all followers of Jesus, to proclaim the message of God's salvation in Jesus Christ to the whole world.

Ultimately, then, in Jesus Christ there is neither Jew nor Gentile, for all are one in Christ. God's primary concern is for a people, not a piece of real estate. Even if God is planning something special for Israel, it is clear to Sam Habib that it will be an era of reconciliation, justice and peace for all who live in the Middle East.

Sam Habib maintains that in declaring all people who confess Jesus Christ to be the new Israel, God is not denying his people Israel the right to be heirs and joint-heirs with Christ. The apostle Paul makes clear that the doors of salvation are open to the people of Israel to believe in Jesus Christ and come to him as Lord and Saviour.

Western Christians particularly, should not spend their time speculating on when Christ will return; only the Father knows when that will happen. That is made very clear in the gospels, particularly the gospel of Matthew. Even Jesus himself said he did not know when the end would come and refused to speculate when the disciples asked him to tell them when the Kingdom of Israel would be restored. It was not his business to second-guess God.

It is the good news that Samuel Habib, tireless prophet of hope, spends his waking hours working to achieve.

So when American Christians give their uncritical support to Israel we have to ask: Where is the moral vision of the church of Jesus Christ? We cannot have double standards. God is for justice, peace and human rights for all people. We must have only one set of standards, applicable to Jews and Arabs alike, and not elevate Israel as a nation above other nations.

Sam Habib acknowledges that none of the nations in the Middle East is blameless in their actions towards one another. In the West, Christians especially must remain sensitive to a hostile anti-Semitism that often lurks just beneath the surface, and remember that most Jews, especially those living in Israel, live in the shadow of the Holocaust.

At the same time, Jews in Palestine cannot ignore God's demands for justice for all people and equal human rights. The West cannot sanction militarism and oppression by Israel towards the Arabs under its occupation.

Samuel Habib sees God's concern for all the oppressed peoples of the earth. There is no Biblical basis for favouring Israel over other nations of the world, and it is important to hold Israel to Biblical standards of justice, just as we must hold neighbouring Arab nations who deny religious freedom for some of their people, degrade women, and maintain an autocratic style of government, to the same standards.

Christians in the West should nevertheless side with the suffering people of Palestine, just as Jesus sided with the suffering and the oppressed of his day. Jesus stands with those who suffer from sickness, oppression and homelessness, and so must we.

Chapter 11

The Way Forward

The way forward demands a brief look back.

To begin to understand the religious and political complexities of the Middle East, Dr. Samuel Habib sees human rights as the central and fundamental issue.

The Palestinian problem of the past forty-five years has been largely one of human rights. The Balfour Treaty of 1917 which allowed Israel to be established as a nation in that part of the Middle East also led to the dispossession of its Palestinian residents.

During the same period Egypt became increasingly committed to the Arab cause in Palestine, but its unexpected defeat in the first Arab-Israeli war (1948–49) contributed to disillusionment and political unrest.

In 1956 Israel, Britain and France went to war against Egypt over the Egyptian nationalization of the Suez Canal. In the early Sixties the PLO was founded. In 1967 Egypt again went to war with Israel, which ended decisively with the defeat of Egypt at the Suez Canal. International pressure brought about an end to the war and President Nasser retreated.

The war that erupted between Egypt and Israel in 1973 was initiated by President Anwar Sadat. In it Egypt regained a portion of the Sinai Peninsula lost to the Israelis in 1967. In the Eighties, under President Hosni Mubarak, Egypt recovered the rest of Sinai, not by war but through peace accords achieved by negotiations led by then President Anwar Sadat, U.S. President Jimmy Carter and Israeli Prime Minister Menachem Begin.

But it has been the ongoing struggle between Israel and the Palestinian people that continues to pose the greatest obstacle and threat to long-term peace in the Middle East. With new outline peace accords struck in 1993 between PLO leader Arafat and Israeli

Prime Minister Rabin, with President Clinton urging the two sides on, there is now for the first time real hope for peace.

But is peace really possible? Only time will tell. Whether or not the mutual recognition agreement between the government of Israel and the Palestine Liberation Organization leads to permanent Palestinian statehood is still open. The accords do nonetheless enshrine the principle that the Palestinians are, in fact, a distinct people, defined by the land they call home and entitled to determine their own destiny.

With new political lines drawn and self-rule for Palestinians in the Gaza Strip and on the West Bank a reality, the Palestinian problem is slowly on its way to resolution. Israel must be allowed to live at peace with all her Arab neighbours. In return the Palestinians will have a homeland and a measure of authentic self-government.

Samuel Habib applauds the Camp David accords which brought about a normalization of relations between his nation and Israel and eventually full diplomatic ties between them.

He sees the importance of Israel being at total peace with all her Arab neighbours, and treaties being struck so that the solutions recently outlined for the Palestinian people can be solidified forever.

The Palestinians now have a piece of land that they can call their own, a homeland where they can live at peace and on an equal footing with both Israel and their Arab neighbours, with fully secure borders. Legally binding treaties and fixed boundaries in the process of being politically hammered out will ensure Israel's security and her ability to live in peace with all her neighbours.

Samuel Habib believes that in trading land for peace the Palestinians can now regain their humanity and dignity and live as full human beings, self-governing and subservient to no one.

On the issue of Jerusalem problems remain. Samuel Habib believes the Holy City must remain the centre for all three religions – Jewish, Christian and Muslim – with easy access for all to worship. He believes that some kind of agreement must be struck that will allow all three religions to coexist peacefully.

Egypt, for much of its history, has shown how Christians and Muslims can coexist, with the rights of the minority being respected. An example of this can be found in the literature work of CEOSS. CEOSS's publishing house has the freedom to publish whatever literature it wants and to distribute it freely to whomever will receive it. As a Christian publisher, CEOSS can and does advertise its literature on television and in the secular press. Al-Ahram agency, one of the largest secular distribution agencies in Egypt, distributes the Christian publications of CEOSS.

In the area of Christian worship, Christians in Egypt are free to preach and worship as long as they do so within a church building. The church can add to its membership, and run its activities; however they may not publicly proclaim their faith to or evangelize Muslims.

In the area of social ministry Christians have full freedom to carry on their programmes without interference from the authorities. Church schools and church organizations in Egypt have the freedom to teach their curricula within the limits and regulations of the educational curriculum set by the government for all schools, Muslim and Christian alike. Church- related hospitals are among the finest in Egypt and operate without restrictions of any kind.

As he looks at the total picture of the church in Egypt, Samuel Habib sees tremendous success but also much failure. What all denominations and churches need, he believes, is intelligent, educated leadership, prophetic voices that will carry the church through the end of this century and into the 21st Century.

While there is spiritual renewal going on, the churches have not been growing fast enough in recent years to develop the kind of leadership the church will need to carry it forward in an uncertain environment. While Protestant, Catholic and Orthodox have been, since the Seventies, developing new programmes and covering much new ground both socially and spiritually, Samuel Habib sees a dearth of prophetic leadership emerging.

Most of CEOSS's top staff go abroad at one time or another to do graduate work, mostly in the United States. What they learn about community development, human resources, international relations and theology will form the basic outlook for CEOSS into the next century.

Samuel Habib is troubled by the churches' lack of consistency in managing to work together. If the Christian community would co-operate more in its joint efforts to relieve the suffering of the poor and preach the gospel, it would see a renewal of church life and the revitalization of church membership. Sadly, the churches do not cooperate enough, and more often than not they do the same work separately from each other, thereby duplicating a lot of unnecessary effort.

The churches in Egypt need to look to the future, says Sam, and they can only do this confidently if they are prepared to bury their differences and work together.

In the world at large the two great demons of recent history; Communism and Fascism have disappeared. The democratization of the world, with the emergence of new independent nation states, is inevitable. But the struggle between rich and poor will always continue; there is no abatement there.

Samuel Habib has a vision; a vision of hope, a vision that will not easily die. He has seen too much, lived through too much, and struggled deeply with most of the major social and spiritual issues of the day.

Despite his years he continues the struggle, laying down his life each day in service for his Master, and reaching out with helping hands to those who live their lives along the valley of the Nile.

Epilogue

The heightening tension in Middle East politics was recently brought home to the United States in the single most destructive act of terrorism ever committed on American soil by a group of radical Egyptian Muslim Fundamentalists.

A large strategically-placed bomb in the basement of the twin towers of the World Trade Centre in Manhattan, New York City exploded, killing seven people, injuring thousands more and resulting in business losses totalling more than $1 billion.

The bombers were followers of New Jersey-based, radical Egyptian Fundamentalist cleric, Sheik Omar Abdel-Rahman, spiritual leader of the Islamic Jihad, or Holy War, whose name has been linked with the assassination of Egyptian President Anwar Sadat in 1981.

Despite the fact that the blind cleric has less than 100 followers in Egypt and certainly does not speak for millions of Muslims, such violence touches the very heart of the tensions between Arab and Jew in the volatile world of the Middle East.

It is the one troubling aspect of Middle East life that keeps Dr. Samuel Habib, the gentle Protestant Christian leader constantly on the move, building support for a peaceful coalition of religious forces in his country.

The clock is running out for Egypt and only God knows when the final curtain of history will be drawn. But until that day dawns, Samuel Habib, visionary Christian, leader, ecumenist and prophet will tread the earth in search of peace, a man of vision with a vision of hope.